MW01004262

JAM

# The Little Big COOKBOOK for MOMS

By Alice Wong & Natasha Tabori Fried

welcome BOOKS
NEW YORK

# Table of Contents

## SOUPS & SANDWICHES



## SNACKS & SMALL BITES

## VEGGIES & SIDES

## DESSERTS

# Forewords

The most frequently asked question in my family is "What's for dinner?" While my girls—ages nine, thirteen, and fifteen—might feel otherwise at times, they are very, very lucky in the eating department. Both my husband and I cook a wide repertoire of foods influenced by personal taste and cultural upbringing, and the fact that we work on cookbooks and test recipes means that the girls are exposed to a worldly array of dishes. I can just imagine the stories they'll tell when they are older: "Remember the time Mom was testing recipes for that butcher cookbook and we had strange meats for dinner for months?" "And what about that time when Dad was testing mac 'n' cheese and used the baba ganoush Mom made instead of the cheese? We had mac a'noush for dinner!"

Between stints of recipe testing, my husband and I make the tried and true at home. My tastes lean toward the simple and clean dishes I grew up with. My childhood meals were often vegetable stir-fries with a bit of meat or steamed fish, lightly blanched greens, and fresh fruit. I still prefer unfussy dishes where the main ingredients are allowed to shine. My favorite recipes in this book are the Broiled Salmon, Chicken with Garlic and Shallots, Quinoa with Fennel, and practically all the vegetable dishes. I love vegetables. My girls know they are lucky, because Dad cooks—and their favorite meals are from him! Clark loves saucier dishes with an explosion of flavors. Unlike me, he is not put off by a longer list of ingredients. Turkey Meatballs with Linguine, Southwestern Chicken Tacos, and Vegetable Lasagna are his trusty dinner favorites.

But as all moms know, dinners are only part of the story. Kids can eat A LOT! No sooner is lunch off the table on weekends than they are scrounging around for a snack, and on weekdays they come home ravenous after school or sports. Snacks are huge in a growing kid's life, and over the years I've learned to be prepared. Stocking the cupboards and refrigerator with prepackaged, somewhat-healthy snacks takes a huge chunk out of a food budget, however. Making and freezing little bites like empanadas, quiches, and frittatas to reheat, or having beans, hard-boiled eggs, avocados, and salsa handy to make salads or dips is much cheaper. Paying almost $6.00 for a small bag of granola at the health food store makes no sense, when I can easily make 4 quarts of the stuff at a fraction of the cost, by tossing rolled oats, nuts, and dried fruits into the oven.

Feeding a family is expensive, especially if you want to buy organic as often as possible, which I do. Luckily, many of the warehouse clubs are stocking more organics nowadays, and it's easier than ever to find, for example, a 3-pack of organic chicken or a 5-pound bag of frozen organic vegetables at a decent price. For economy, nutrition, and taste, dried beans are a must-have for every family's pantry—along with a slow cooker to make life easier. Rice and Beans, Tuscan Bean Soup, and Quick Bean Salad are regulars at my table. The chart on page 266 is a great guide for testing bean varieties.

Smart-shopping Moms (and Dads) know when to economize and when to spend a little more on the freshest, most delicious local produce. Nothing beats the seasonal apples, sugar snap peas, and asparagus we get at the farmers' market. On Saturday mornings, my husband loves taking my youngest daughter, Phoebe, to our market at Grand Army Plaza in Brooklyn. Besides fresh produce, we indulge in fresh fish from local waters. (When the fish is fresh, the simplest preparation is best, as in our favorites Steamed Whole Fish or Pan-Fried Fish.) Farmers' markets are a wondrous thing in big cities: not only a way to keep in touch with the earth through growing and picking seasons, but also a way to get the kids interested in all the wonderful, colorful vegetables available. If you live near a vegetable farm, that's even better . . . there is something so satisfying about harvesting your own vegetables for dinner.

Recently, we spent an early fall weekend with Natasha at her mom Lena's place on Long Island and visited a CSA farm. Natasha's little boy just turned two and my girls chased him around the rows of vegetables and fruits. We picked squash, okra, and lettuces, searched for late-season berries, and dug for potatoes. At one point, Natasha's son was toddling around chewing on a big piece of raw green pepper Phoebe had picked for him. He flashed a big green grin. That evening, Lena made her simply delicious Pan-Fried Fish with lemon-caper sauce, I made Quinoa and Fennel, and Natasha tossed together a salad of greens and roasted some veggies. We sat outside with the 4 kids, ages 2 to 15, who ate as heartily as the adults. It was divine. I wish you and your family many as happy and healthy a meal.

—A.W.

I've always been a baker. I am the one who never missed the chance to volunteer dessert for the dinner party or cupcakes for the office party. I even made my own wedding cake! But I won't claim to be a great cook. Which is why, when my son hit 8 months and started eating solids, I felt a bit challenged. The ironic part is, making my own baby food was easy. Steam and purée—even I could do it. It got a LOT harder when we got past the purées. He's not a bad eater, but he's a discerning one, and unlike my husband, he's not wild about my simple cooking. Or at least, he's not wild about trying it. Hard to know if he'd like it if he tasted it, but I keep telling him he will. So, in an effort to move beyond mac 'n' cheese, fish sticks, and spinach shapes (all organic, but still!) I've decided to branch out. Alice's kids were eating sushi at a year old, so why shouldn't mine?

We started with all things eggs: scrambled, in quiche, in fritattas (yes, he'll actually eat vegetables this way). Then stews and casseroles, and finally, I even made my first risotto! It wasn't nearly as hard as I had feared: in fact, as my little one gets older it will be a good dish to make with him, since he can take over all the stirring. And both he and my husband loved it. Once I'd tackled that, vegetables were simple. I discovered that roasted veggies are ridiculously easy and delicious. The Sautéed Cabbage and the Quick Cabbage Slaw are both very popular in my house.

What I've learned is that cooking healthy, yummy food for my family isn't hard (phew) as long as I'm not a perfectionist, but that cooking for little ones who are learning, exploring, and testing what they can control can be. The trick is to keep trying new things and old ones, because sooner or later they just might decide they like it, not just yesterday, but always. Eating meals with family and friends, especially with older kids, help a lot as well. Little ones will be curious and excited to eat what the big kids eat.

There is so much to learn as a parent, and my first two years with my son has been a breathtaking and satisfying journey. He can walk down the street now, holding my hand. I tell him how nice it is and he brings my hand up to rub against his cheek in response. Of course my heart melts, and, of course, I want the best of everything for him. I look forward to real conversations, reading all the childhood classics together, and him starting school . . . but most of all I want to watch him grow up healthy and strong. Cooking well and trying out new foods requires some thought and a lot of patience, but that's part of it all. I'm a mom now!

**—N.T.F**

# General Nutrition

Our culture does not make it easy to raise a healthy child. The media is constantly bombarding children with ads for candy and sugary snacks. Fast-food restaurants offer salty, fatty foods that appeal to taste buds and are served with toys. Teaching your child to eat nutritiously may be a long, challenging process, but it's well worth it. Children need to eat a variety of foods, including protein, carbohydrates, fruits, and vegetables—it's essential to their growth. Be a role model. If children see their parents buying and enjoying nutritious food, they are more likely to do so themselves. Create a pleasant, unhurried environment around the breakfast, lunch, and dinner table. Keep a variety of easily accessible nutritious snacks—a raw vegetable tray or fresh fruit salad on a low refrigerator shelf, or nuts, whole-grain crackers and pretzels, and rice cakes in a low cupboard. Show your child how to recognize foods that support growth and those that don't. Explain that different foods help them grow in different ways. "If you eat yogurt, you'll have strong, healthy bones and teeth." Teach older children how to read and interpret nutrition labels. Keep a pitcher of water—the most vital drink of all—where children can reach it. Be patient—learning to eat healthy doesn't happen overnight.

# Glossary of Essentials

All essential nutrients needed by you and your growing children can be found in a varied, well-balanced diet.

**AMINO ACIDS** are the building blocks of protein. The body creates about half of the twenty types of amino acids (the nonessential amino acids); the rest, the essential amino acids, must be supplied by diet.

**ANTIOXIDANTS** help protect the body and decrease the risk of cancer and many chronic diseases. A variety of whole foods, such as fruits, vegetables, nuts, grains, and beans will supply a wide range of antioxidants.

**CARBOHYDRATES** are the body's primary source of energy. Complex carbohydrates are energy-rich foods, including whole-grain cereals, breads, pastas, and rice. These foods retain vitamins, minerals, and fiber, unlike their refined counterparts, such as white bread or most store-bought cookies.

**PROTEIN** is needed for growth and repair of our body tissues. Our bodies don't store protein naturally, so it's important to eat foods containing protein every day. While animal proteins provide all the amino acids the body needs, most other protein sources need to be combined with other foods to provide complete protein. Serve whole grains with legumes or beans for complete protein.

**FATS** are especially important for the littlest ones in your family—they're essential for children's growth. Babies up to age one need as much as 50 percent of their energy intake from fat. Children between two and five need up to 35 percent. Fats fall into two basic categories: saturated and unsaturated.

**Saturated fats:** are solid at room temperature. They are primarily found in animal and dairy products, although some vegetable products, such as coconut and palm oils, are also saturated fats. Once in the bloodstream, saturated fats become the forerunners of low-density lipoproteins (LDL), or "bad cholesterol," which can inhibit blood flow and contribute to heart disease and some forms of cancer.

**Unsaturated fats:** are liquid at room temperature. They include fish, vegetable, and nut oils that do not contribute to bad cholesterol, heart disease, or cancer. Some studies have shown that these kinds of fats can actually lower LDL (bad) cholesterol and maintain HDL (good) cholesterol.

**FIBER**, or roughage, is the indigestible portion of plant foods that helps prevent constipation, lowers cholesterol, slows the absorption of sugar, and supports the immune system. Fruits, vegetables, whole grains, and legumes are good sources of fiber.

**MINERALS** help proteins, fats, and carbohydrates produce energy. They work with vitamins to maintain metabolism, prevent disease, and continue healthy body processes. The body needs some minerals, like calcium, in large quantities, and other minerals, like chromium and selenium, in small quantities. Some important minerals:

**Calcium:** Good for healthy teeth, bones, nerves, muscles, and heart tissue. Sources: milk, yogurt, cheese, leafy vegetables, tofu, nuts, sardines, and sesame seeds.

**Iron:** carries oxygen from the lungs to all body cells and promotes mental and physical development. Sources: liver, red meat, oily fish, legumes, green leafy vegetables, dried apricots, and raisins.

**Magnesium:** Supports absorption of calcium. Good for nerves, muscles, bones, and blood circulation. Sources: Spinach, chard, and some types of seeds, legumes, and fish.

**Potassium:** Good for muscles, nerves, and maintenance of normal blood pressure. Sources: chard, spinach, avocados, and some legumes.

**Zinc:** Good for growth, immune system, and the metabolism of protein and fatty acids. Sources: red meat, shellfish, sunflower seeds, and peanuts.

**OMEGA-3 FATTY ACIDS** occur in polyunsaturated fat and are good for the brain, nervous system, and heart. They are found in oily fish (like salmon and sardines), flaxseeds, and, to a lesser degree, eggs (from chickens fed omega-3s), walnuts, and some leafy green vegetables.

**VITAMINS** keep us healthy. Heat destroys water-soluble vitamins, such as B and C, so it's best to avoid overcooking vegetables or fruits that are high in these vitamins. Fat-soluble vitamins A, D, E, and K stay stored in the body and can be harmful in large doses.

**Vitamin A:** Good for eyesight, growth, appetite, making red blood cells, and taste. Sources: Carrots, red peppers, tomatoes, sweet potatoes, mangoes, apricots, corn, liver, fish-liver oil, eggs, green leafy vegetables, and milk products.

**B-complex Vitamins:** include thiamine, riboflavin, niacin, and folic acid. Good for nervous system, digestion, growth, muscles, heart, skin, nails, hair, and eyesight. Sources: liver, yeast, rice, peanuts, pork, chicken, milk, cheese, green leafy vegetables, tofu, sardines, eggs, whole-grain cereals, avocados, bananas, and dried beans.

**Vitamin C:** Good for growth, the immune system, protection from bacteria and viruses, tissue repair, cell lifespan, lowering cholesterol, and aiding in iron absorption. Sources: kiwi fruit, citrus fruits, strawberries, dark green leafy vegetables, peppers, and potatoes.

**Vitamin D:** Good for strong bones and teeth and absorbing calcium and phosphorous. Sources: sunlight, cod-liver oil, salmon, sardines, tuna, herring, milk products, cheese, and eggs.

**Vitamin E:** Good for fighting poisons and for maintaining healthy cell structure and red blood cells. Sources: nuts, avocados, soybeans, vegetable oils, broccoli, spinach, whole-grain products, and eggs.

**Vitamin K:** Good for normal blood clotting and regulation of calcium levels in the blood. Sources: spinach, kale, collards, broccoli, soybean oil, olive oil, and canola oil.

## Dietary Guidance

The U.S. Department of Agriculture recommends that fully half our meal should comprise fruits and vegetables, while the grain and protein portions should each occupy about a quarter of the plate. The USDA further admonishes us to use whole grains for the grain portion, as opposed to refined breads, white rice, and white flour. A third key point is the recommendation for milk as a part of the separate dairy portion.

How much of each? From toddlers to seniors, depending on your age, sex, and activity level, the USDA recommends eating the following per day: veggies, 1½ to 3 cups or more; fruits, 1 to 2 cups or more; grains (whole-grain sources), 1½ to 4 servings*; dairy, 2 to 3 cups; and protein, 2 to 6½ servings max.

* A serving equals 1 ounce equivalent, defined by the USDA as 1 slice of bread, 1 cup of ready-to-eat cereal, or ½ cup of cooked rice, cooked pasta, or cooked cereal, for grains; or 1 ounce of lean meat, poultry or fish, ¼ cup cooked beans, 1 egg, 1 tablespoon of peanut butter, or ½ ounce of nuts or seeds, for protein.

For more information, look up dietary guidelines at www.usda.gov.

# Making Choices

**As a mom, you are in charge of your child's health—at least when it comes to nutrition. You have control over what type of food you keep in your kitchen. You decide whether to buy whole foods, organic foods, or processed foods. You know about good nutrition, or if you don't, you have the ability to learn. Your child does not have the knowledge and understanding you do. Children often go for candy, ice cream, and other sugary snacks, which provide instant gratification. Prohibiting your child from having any junk food can be tricky, but there are ways to compromise. Become familiar with reading and understanding food labels—some "junk" foods are better than others. Explain to your child that you want her to eat well because you care about her, so she won't feel deprived. If your child wants a candy bar or sugary drink that you don't want her to have, don't be afraid to say no. Offer her some naturally sweet fruit or a smoothie instead. Remind yourself that when it comes to nutrition, Mom knows best.**

## THINK WHOLE FOODS

The best way to get the most out of the food we eat is to include a wide variety of whole foods—grains, legumes, nuts, seeds, and fresh fruits and vegetables—in our diet. Natural foods are the best sources of vitamins, fiber, minerals, complex carbohydrates, fats, and nutrients necessary for healthy physical and mental function.

Be on the lookout for processed foods containing questionable additives, preservatives, chemicals, artificial ingredients, and unwanted sugar, sodium, or saturated fat. Many of these additives can have adverse health effects.

## CHOOSE ORGANIC WHEN POSSIBLE

Commercially grown produce is sprayed with legal amounts of toxic pesticides, which interfere with the way the body processes nutrients. Some farmers use sewage sludge to fertilize their crops. In addition to human waste, this sludge can contain toxic chemicals, cleaners, and heavy metals.

Another concern is the use of antibiotics. From 60 to 80 percent of all cattle, sheep, and poultry in the United States will receive antibiotics at some point. The commercial dairy business is dominated by huge farms where cows are machine-milked, confined to the barnyard, fed hay and grain grown in fields sprayed with pesticides, and routinely given antibiotics to combat diseases. A large proportion—20 to 30 percent—of these cows are given hormones. Organic food is grown without synthetic fertilizers, pesticides, herbicides, hormones, or antibiotics, and reduces the risk of getting cancer or other diseases. (See also pages 188 and 248.)

## WATCH FATS

You may want to think twice before buying another bag of goldfish, box of animal crackers, or box of cereal at your local supermarket. Read the labels and you'll find many contain partially hydrogenated fat, as do doughnuts, fast-food French fries, microwave popcorn, soft-serve ice cream, graham crackers, granola bars, and commercially made baked goods. Partially hydrogenated fat is a vegetable fat that's been bombarded with hydrogen to make it solid at room temperature—a big advantage to processed-food makers. It solidifies liquid margarine to give it a longer shelf life. When a food contains partially hydrogenated fat, it contains trans fat, an artificial fat manufactured to imitate naturally saturated fats. There is evidence that trans fats predispose children to diabetes, obesity, and cancer, and stimulate insulin overproduction.

Read labels. You may find certain brands do not use partially hydrogenated oil. Otherwise, shop at health-food stores.

## REDUCE SUGAR

Carbohydrates provide our bodies with their best source of fuel. Sugars are simple carbohydrates. When we eat sugar in its natural state, such as in fresh fruits and starches—or complex carbohydrates—it is diluted and coexists with fiber and other nutrients necessary for digestion and healthy brain function.

The problem with consuming refined sugars is that they give us energy without significant nutritional value. Table sugar, brown sugar, molasses, honey, and powdered sugar contain roughly between 50 and 100 calories per tablespoon. We may think that eating empty calories is okay if we burn them off with physical activity, but in fact we are robbing our bodies of existing vitamins and minerals in order to digest these empty calories. Reducing simple sugars will significantly decrease your family's health risks related to obesity and malnutrition.

### REDUCE SODIUM

Sodium is an essential mineral for the body, necessary for healthy muscle and nerve function and for regulating the body's water balance. The typical American diet contains far more sodium than is necessary, which is generally less than a teaspoon per day. Be on the lookout for high-sodium foods, such as canned soups, cured meats, packaged snack foods, pickled foods, processed cheeses, dehydrated mixes, and fast foods. Too much sodium can put the ones you love on an unhealthy path toward hypertension (high blood pressure), heart attack, stroke, and kidney disease.

### TO SUPPLEMENT OR NOT?

Vitamins, minerals, probiotics, fish oil, antioxidant pills, blue-green algae. Because these supplements straddle the line between nutritional and medicinal, they've earned the moniker "nutraceuticals." But do they really add life to our years and make our families healthier? Indeed, a simple blood test can show that calcium pills raise calcium levels, but how much of that calcium do our bodies use efficiently to build or maintain bone density? And what is the correct amount of the vitamin D most of us are deficient in, anyway? The answers are complicated.

Staying on the calcium topic, take whole milk as an example. Formerly known as a perfect food but falling out of favor in the past few years, it is now staging a comeback. Warnings against whole milk's fat content are being questioned by health experts. When you take all the fat out of milk, you are left with too high a concentration of natural sugars. The fat in milk binds with its calcium, which also links up with fat from other foods, making whole milk, despite the calories, unlikely to cause clogged arteries when consumed in moderation. Moderation is a key aspect of supplementation, too. Experts say that the fewer pills you take, the less likely you are to run into problems caused by lots of different additives from lots of different pills. Use common sense: discuss supplementation with your pediatrician and concentrate on meeting nutritional needs through diet. Choose foods wisely: fruit instead of candy, milk instead of soda, whole-grain bread instead of salty chips. Don't forget: in moderation.

## BE AWARE OF BPA

Bisphenol A, or BPA, is a chemical that occurs in the manufacture of many types of plastic containers, baby bottles, cups, and the linings of metal food and beverage cans. Trace amounts of BPA have been found in the foods they hold. Since the FDA's 2008 proclamation of BPA's safety, questions have been raised as to its properties as an "endocrine-disruptive" substance—questions that the federal government is now taking seriously. BPA exposure is considered most problematic in very young children, whose bodies' ability to detoxify is not fully developed.

Strive for a low-BPA household. When possible, prepare and store foods—especially hot foods—in glass, ceramic, or stainless-steel containers. Do not use plastic containers in the microwave. Use packaged foods that come in shelf-stable cartons or boxes, or are from manufacturers, like Eden Foods, that line cans with a BPA alternative. Buy tuna in pouches, use dried soups, and eat fresh or frozen veggies. Another source of BPA is in dental sealants. Some older versions of dental sealants contain the chemical, and some dentists prefer them.

SARDINES
SOAP.

# Top 10 Ways
## to Get Your Child to Eat Better

1 TAKE TIME TO INTRODUCE NEW FOODS: Children's taste buds aren't always ready for new flavors or textures. Be patient if your son or daughter shows resistance to trying new foods. Introduce a new food again at a later date or sneak it into a dish that you know they already love. Of course, revealing that a favorite relative, celebrity, or hero likes spinach can work wonders to get your tot to try it.

2 BREAK THAT FAST: Breakfast is the most important meal of the day—make it count. You can prepare whole-grain waffles on the weekend and freeze them for the coming week. Pop them in the toaster oven in the mornings and top with fresh fruit, yogurt, and honey for a quick, delicious, and nutritious way to start the day.

3 PLAN AHEAD: Keep your pantry packed with basic staples that make it easy to whip up nutritious meals. Think about variations on whole-grain pasta, bread, or rice; sautéed, steamed or fresh vegetables; and a protein source such as tofu, poultry, meat, fish, cheese, or beans. Casseroles, stews, and chili are also easy ways to serve a balanced meal in a single dish.

4 ENCOURAGE YOUNG COOKS: As your children grow, encourage them to participate in shopping for, preparing, and creating meals. When kids can be creative in the kitchen, they'll naturally show more interest in what they're eating.

5 DRESS IT UP: If your children aren't excited about fruits and vegetables, try creative sauces, hummus, and salsas. Blend plain yogurt with seasonings for dipping vegetables or fruit (page 144). Try salad dressings on raw veggies (page 201). Make smoothies or blended fruits (pages 58 and 63).



6 PACK A PICNIC: If you know that you'll be spending a fair amount of time driving the kids to and from school and extracurricular activities, maintain a cooler in the car to keep the munchies (and grumpies) at bay. Stock it with fresh-chopped veggies, nuts, granola, yogurt, water, apples, and bananas.

7 DON'T MAKE A FUSS: Try to resist making comments on what or how much your children are eating. As long as you are doing your part to serve them balanced and nutritious meals, the rest is up to the kids. Telling them to finish every bite of their dinner may end up creating resistance rather than compliance.

8 CREATE SIMPLE, FLEXIBLE MENUS: Don't get trapped into making separate meals for all the members of your family. Plan menus that you can serve family style, and allow your children to choose what they want to eat. Eventually, they may follow your example to sample everything.

9 HAVE A HEALTHY ATTITUDE: Your approach to diet, health, exercise, and lifestyle sets an example for your children. If you skip meals or make unbalanced choices, your kids may think that's okay for them, too. By listening to your body to tell you when you're full or hungry, your children will learn to do the same.

10 MAKE FOOD TIME A FUN TIME: Get creative in the kitchen. You can turn a morning of pancakes into a smiley-face contest. Cut and arrange sandwiches to represent different animals. Make a meal of just mini foods or try serving "breakfast" for dinner. And take on ideas from your kids—your enthusiasm will be infectious.

# A Perfect Pantry

**When you don't have time to plan ahead for dinner or don't want to shop for food in inclement weather, a well-stocked pantry and refrigerator can be a godsend. Purchase extra dried and packaged ingredients for your family's favorite meals. Then, when you're in a pinch, you can still whip up waffles and smoothies for breakfast, or jazz up plain pasta with an herb sauce.**

## STAPLES

Beans (chickpeas, lima, kidney, pinto, black)
Breakfast cereals
Bouillon cubes: chicken and beef
Broth: chicken and beef
Dried fruits
Grains (quinoa, millet, kasha, couscous)
Nuts (walnuts, almonds, cashews, pine nuts)
Oil (extra-virgin olive oil, canola, sesame)
Packaged and instant soups (tomato, chicken noodle, vegetable)
Pasta varieties
Popcorn
Powdered milk for emergencies
Rice
Split peas
Tomatoes
Trail mix
Tuna
Vinegar (red, white, balsamic, rice)

---

## BAKING SUPPLIES

Baking powder
Baking soda
Bread crumbs
Cornstarch
Dried fruits
Evaporated milk
Extracts (vanilla, almond, orange)
Flours (whole-wheat flour, barley flour, buckwheat, cornmeal)
Honey
Powdered milk
Rolled oats
Salt
Sugars (white, brown, confectioners', raw)
Wheat germ
Yeast

### CONDIMENTS

Butter
Garlic
Ginger
Herbs (see pages 34–35)
Horseradish
Jam or jelly
Ketchup
Maple syrup
Mayonnaise
Mustard
Peanut butter
Peppercorns
Relishes
Salsas
Soy sauce, low-sodium
Spices (see pages 34–35)
Tomato paste
Tomato sauce
Worcestershire sauce

### IN THE FREEZER

Bread
Chicken breasts
English muffins or tortillas
Frozen fruits (berries and peeled bananas for smoothies)
Frozen juice bars
Frozen juice concentrate
Frozen vegetables (lima beans, peas, corn, spinach, soybeans)
Frozen waffles
Ground beef or turkey
Homemade broth
Pork tenderloins
Tortellini or ravioli

(See page 38 for freezing guidelines)

### IN THE FRIDGE

Apples
Baby carrots
Cheeses (mozzarella, parmesan, string)
Celery
Cream cheese
Eggs
Fresh fruits
Hummus
Juice
Milk
Yogurt

### FAVORITE EXTRAS

Applesauce
Bottled pasta sauce
Brownie mixes
Cake and muffin mixes
Chocolate chips
Cocoa/chocolate drink mix
Fig bars
Gelatin
Hot cereals
Macaroni and cheese
Munchies: pretzels, breadsticks, crackers
Pancake mix
Rice cakes

# Herbs and Spices

| | | |
|---|---|---|
| BAY LEAVES | Added whole during cooking of hearty stews, sauces, soups for extra depth of flavor; crushed in marinades; powdered in rubs. | Store in a tightly sealed container in a cool, dark place; whole: 1 year; crushed or powdered: several months. |
| BLACK PEPPER | Works in almost any dish that needs a hot sweetness, even some desserts; add whole to sauces, chicken, cracked to coat steaks, fish, roasts (ground has poor flavor). | Store in a tightly sealed container in a cool, dark place; whole: at least 1 year; cracked: 6 months; ground: not recommended; grind your own! |
| CHILI POWDER | Use in chili, tacos, meat loaf, salad dressings, rubs; varieties range from very mild to hot. | Store in a tightly sealed container in a cool, dark, dry place for up to 6 months. |
| CUMIN | Use in chili, Tex-Mex, Indian curries, in rubs for beef, chicken, and pork. | Store in a tightly sealed container in a cool, dark place; whole seeds: 2 years; ground: 1 year; fresh: a few days in the refrigerator. |
| DILL WEED | Use in pickling, seafood salads, sauces; dried is six times as potent as fresh and stands up to cooking. | Store dried in a tightly sealed container in a cool, dry place for 6 months. |

| | | |
|---|---|---|
| NUTMEG | Use a pinch in eggnog, spice cakes and other baked goods, soufflés, spinach, creamed potatoes. | Store in a tightly sealed container in a cool place; whole: keeps indefinitely; ground: several months. |
| PAPRIKA | Sprinkle on deviled eggs, chicken, pot roast, potatoes, fish to add color or peppery flavor. | Store in a tightly sealed container in a cool, dark place for up to 6 months. |
| ROSEMARY | Adds pinelike fragrance, pungent flavor, and more than 80 nutrients to Mediterranean dishes, chicken, lamb, pork, salmon, tuna. Whole fresh sprigs can be cooked and removed before serving. | Store fresh (preferred), wrapped in moist paper towel several days in refrigerator; dried, in a tightly sealed container in a cool, dark, dry place for 6 months. |
| SAGE | Use in rich meat dishes, stuffings, poultry, pork, biscuits (the dried form is more potent than fresh sage, so use with discretion.) Longer cooking time reduces its "bite." | Store fresh (preferred), wrapped in moist paper towel several days in refrigerator; dried, in a tightly sealed container in a cool, dark, dry place for 6 months. |
| TARRAGON | Main herb in classic French cooking, Béarnaise sauce, chicken, seafood; fresh is more potent than dried. | Store fresh, refrigerated, 2 to 3 days; frozen in an airtight bag 3 to 5 months; dried, 1 year. |
| THYME | Use for lamb, tomato sauces, egg dishes, stews; with other herbs; stronger when dried. | Store fresh, a few days in the refrigerator; dried, tightly sealed in a container in a cool, dark place, 6 months to a year. |

# Food Safety & Storage

**When it comes to eating right, making food choices is only half the battle. A few simple precautions in the kitchen when handling, preparing, and cooking food can make all the difference between a nutritious meal and unwanted food contamination. Just follow these simple guidelines and the table of suggested cooking temperatures on page 38 for best results.**

## PREPPING & COOKING

- Shop smart (buy freshest food possible, shop in well-maintained stores and markets).
- Clean your work surface before you start.
- Thaw frozen meat in the refrigerator.
- Scrub hands thoroughly before handling food.
- Clean cutting board and knives with soap and water in between use. Use a separate cutting board for raw meats.
- Keep raw, fresh foods refrigerated until you are ready to cook them.
- Prepare thawed foods immediately.
- Never use a dish that hasn't been washed.
- Cook eggs and chicken thoroughly to kill salmonella bacteria. Whole chickens should be heated to 180°F; breasts to 165°F.
- Cook ground beef to an internal temperature of at least 160°F.

## STORING

- Keep cold foods cold and hot foods hot. Bacteria thrive between 40˚F and 140˚F.
- Do not leave cooked food out at room temperature for more than two hours.
- Keep raw meat, poultry, and fish well wrapped in the refrigerator. Drippings can spread bacteria to other foods.

- Do not store leftover canned food in the original can. Check for bulges in cans and jar lids for evidence of bacterial growth.
- Cool hot food before freezing it and, when possible, refrigerate a few hours before freezing. Wrap foods in airtight freezer containers or bags. This prevents freezer burn, protects flavor, and minimizes dehydration.
- Be sure to date and label all foods stored in the freezer. Follow the rule, "first in, first out." Follow the freezing guidelines below.

## FREEZING GUIDELINES

- Vegetables (up to 6 months)
- Fruits (up to 12 months)
- Meats
  - Hamburger (up to 4 months)
  - Hot dogs and lunch meats (up to 2 months)
  - Bacon (up to 1 month)
  - Sausage (up to 1 month)
  - Ham (up to 2 months)
  - Beef steaks and roasts (up to 12 months)
  - Pork chops and roasts (up to 6 months)
  - Lamb roasts (up to 9 months)
  - Cooked meat dishes (up to 3 months)
- Poultry
  - Chicken or turkey, whole (up to 12 months)
  - Chicken or turkey, parts (up to 9 months)
- Fish
  - Fresh fish (up to 3 months)
  - Fatty fish, such as salmon (up to 2 months)
  - Shellfish (up to 2 months)
  - Cooked fish dishes (up to 3 months)
- Dairy
  - Egg whites (up to 12 months)
  - Butter (up to 6 months)
  - Cream (up to 2 months)
  - Milk (up to 1 month)
- Cheese
  - Hard (up to 6 months)
  - Processed (up to 4 months)
- Baked Goods, Breads
  - Quick breads (up to 2 months)
  - Yeast breads (up to 6 months)
  - Yeast dough (up to 2 weeks)
  - Cookie dough (up to 4 months)
  - Unbaked pastry (up to 2 months)
  - Baked pastry (up to 2 months)

# Table of Suggested Cooking Temperatures

| MEAT | INNER DONENESS | INNER TEMPERATURE OF FOOD | | |
|---|---|---|---|---|
| **Beef** | Medium rare | 145°F | or | 63°C |
| | Medium | 160°F | or | 71°C |
| | Well done | 170°F | or | 77°C |
| **Pork** | Medium | 160°F | or | 71°C |
| | Well done | 170°F | or | 77°C |
| **Ham** | Fully cooked | 140°F | or | 64°C |
| **Lamb** | Medium rare | 150°F | or | 66°C |
| | Medium | 160°F | or | 71°C |
| **Turkey** | Breast | 170°F | or | 77°C |
| | Dark meat | 180°F | or | 82°C |
| | Whole (bone in) | 180°–185°F | or | 82°–85°C |
| **Chicken** | Whole pieces (bone in) | 180°F | or | 82°C |
| | Boneless | 165°F | or | 74°C |
| **Duckling** | | 180°–185°F | or | 82°–85°C |

NOTE: Cooked meat should be allowed to rest about 5 to 10 minute before cutting to allow the juices to redistribute. The temperature of the meat will continue to rise a little during resting, about 10°F to 15°F, so remove the meat from the heat a little early.

# Feeding Baby

**Have you caught your baby eyeing your food plate lately? Do you think it might be time for the much anticipated "first meal"? Well, always check with your child's pediatrician before beginning solids, but more than likely it will be around the half-year mark. (Some babies can begin solids around four months of age; however, delaying the start as long as possible will give your baby's digestive system a chance to mature.) Some of the signs that your baby is ready to eat solid food are the fact that she sits without support, has good head and neck control, no longer thrusts her tongue forward, shows interest in food, and is no longer satisfied by 32 ounces of breast milk or formula per day. Don't be surprised if it takes the rest of the first year for your baby to genuinely take to food.**

Starting solids is hard work for your baby. As much as your little one fusses when denied a bite of your tuna-fish sandwich, his first bite of solid food might not bring a smile to his face. Try to be as encouraging as possible. Reassure him and talk to him about how proud you are and how "yummy" it must taste. Taste some yourself to provide security. And during the first few meals, watch carefully for cues that say your baby needs to stop. If the meals don't seem to get off the ground at first, wait a few days and try again. He'll appreciate your patience.

## FIRST FOODS

Single-grain cereals are generally recommended as the first foods for babies. Rice is a great place to start, as it is a highly digestible food. The very first feeding should be one tablespoon of cereal to three tablespoons of liquid, such as expressed breast milk, formula, or water—hardly what you'd call solid! Many pediatricians suggest moving next to puréed vegetables (rather than fruits) in order that babies become accustomed to more subtle flavors. Thin the consistency of these foods with water as well. The foods should drip off the spoon when you tilt it to baby's mouth.



It's perfectly normal, and in fact desirable, for breast milk or formula to remain the core of your baby's diet for the first year (24 to 32 ounces daily).

### GREAT FIRSTS

Plan to spend the first month working through these great firsts: rice cereal, millet cereal, sweet potatoes, avocados, bananas

### 6 MONTHS

Oatmeal, barley cereal, yogurt, squash, pears, peaches, mangoes, papayas, apricots, nectarines, plums, prunes

### 7 MONTHS

Multi-grain cereals, egg yolk, tofu, whole-milk cottage cheese, asparagus, carrots, peas, white potatoes, rice cakes

### 8 MONTHS

Apples, cantaloupe, honeydew, kiwi, broccoli, grapes, cheese, teething biscuits, diluted juices: apple, pear, grape

### 9 MONTHS

Legumes (not peanuts), pineapple, spinach, beets, kale, rutabaga, turnips, whole-grain pasta

### 12 MONTHS+

Grated carrot, whole milk, citrus fruits and juices, tomatoes and tomato juice, egg whites, honey

# Homemade for Baby

We all know that homemade food is the most nutritious fare. This is infinitely truer for babies, when you consider that they must derive a slew of nutrients out of very few calories (approximately 50 calories a day per pound of weight). And though it may not be possible to feed your baby fresh, homemade food every day, you can come close. The trick is in the planning, preparation, and storage. Of course, no one wants to slave away in the kitchen for an hour, only to have the beets you steamed or the cereal you whipped up thrown all over the floor. Here are some tips to help make the food preparation easy enough so it won't matter if a little ends up on Junior's splash mat.

Making just enough puréed carrot to satisfy the tiny appetite of your seven-month-old can be time-consuming. And, when you consider that you'll be doing the same thing for the next three nights à la the four-day trial period, it's enough to have you singing the hot-stove blues. What if there was a way to do it once for all four nights . . . no . . . for six months' worth of carrots for your little rabbit? Well, that's exactly what you can do with the food-cube method. (And while you're at it, you can cook the asparagus, peas, and white potatoes you'll be serving this month.) Suddenly that hour (or so) you are relegated to the kitchen, washing, steaming, straining, or puréeing the veggies, becomes entirely worthwhile.

**Sticking with Month Seven as an example, here is what your "hour" in the kitchen might look like:**

### 1. WASH THOSE VEGGIES (5 TO 10 MINUTES)

Before you start the washing, put some water in your steamer to boil so it will be waiting for you, instead of the other way around. Using a mild soap-and-water solution, gently wash the carrots, asparagus, and potatoes. Peas should only need a quick rinse if they are just shelled. Use a vegetable brush on the carrots and potatoes, but leave the skins on (unless the carrots are very mature and large), as that is where much of the nutrients lie. Do remove any spoiled spots and the eyes, sprouts, and any green areas on the potatoes. Break the tough ends from the bottoms of the asparagus stalks and discard them.

### 2. STEAM THOSE VEGGIES (10 MINUTES)

Add first the coarsely chopped carrots (10 minutes), then the sliced potatoes and shelled peas (8 minutes), and finally the asparagus (5 minutes).

### 3. PURÉE THOSE VEGGIES (10 TO 15 MINUTES)

After your veggies are cooked, separate them out and purée each type in your blender or mini food processor. If you have more than one batch of a vegetable, don't waste time scraping every last bit out between batches. Just pile more food in and keep going.

### 4. FREEZE THOSE VEGGIES (10 TO 15 MINUTES)

After you have removed the portion of vegetables you will need for today's feeding(s), transfer each type of vegetable into ice-cube trays. For beginning eaters, it's a good idea to fill each cube slot only halfway. Later, your child will eat two or three full cubes at each meal. Cover the trays with plastic wrap to prevent freezer burn, and throw the trays in the freezer.

### 5. BAG THOSE VEGGIES

Once your food cubes are frozen, usually after eight or so hours, you should transfer the cubes to plastic freezer bags. Mark each bag with the date you prepared the food. The veggies will keep for up to 6 months but for optimal quality and nutrients, try to use within 3 months.

## Equipment for Feeding Baby

**You don't need much in the way of special equipment to prepare homemade foods for babies. A fine-mesh sieve comes in handy for straining fruits and vegetables for beginning eaters. After your child becomes accustomed to gumming and swallowing foods, you can use a blender for puréeing fruits and vegetables. Alternatively, a mini food processor or hand mill—though not a necessity—that you use only for preparing your baby's food can reduce the risk of cross contamination from other foods. You will also need ice-cube trays and freezer bags. (Make sure the storage bags you buy are specifically for freezing.)**

**In addition to these kitchen supplies, you will need a safe highchair, bibs, and a plastic-coated spoon for those tender gums.**

# Food Allergies

**The chance that your child will have a food allergy of one kind or another is about one in twenty, one in ten if you or your partner have food allergies—not insignificant probabilities when it's your wee one we're talking about. Immediate symptoms may include itchy/swollen throat, sneezing, and watery eyes. (In very rare instances, food can cause anaphylactic shock, in which a child's throat will swell to the point of obstructing breathing and a sharp decrease in blood pressure occurs.) Other symptoms may take up to a few days to surface, and they include skin rashes, stomach cramps, gas, bloating, and diarrhea. The majority of food allergies are caused by the following:**

- Dairy products
- Citrus fruits
- Egg whites
- Peanuts
- Soy products
- Shellfish
- Artificial additives
- Tree nuts (walnuts, cashews, almonds, etc.)
- Wheat

**Less-common culprits:**

- Berries
- Chocolate
- Cinnamon
- Mustard
- Peas
- Pork
- Sugar
- Tomatoes
- Yeast

# Choking Hazards

**According to the American Academy of Pediatrics, children under four years of age are at greatest risk of choking on certain foods. Since infants and young children do not yet grind or chew their food well, round, firm foods that they may attempt to swallow whole are of greatest concern. The following present potential choking hazards:**

- Hot dogs
- Marshmallows
- Ice cubes
- Dried fruit
- Pretzels
- Nuts and seeds
- Chunks of meat or cheese (especially string cheese)
- Pasty globs of bread (lower risk with whole-grain breads)
- Whole grapes
- Hard or sticky candy
- Popcorn
- Chunks of apple
- Peanut butter
- Chips
- Raw vegetables (especially peas, carrots, and celery)
- Whole cooked peas
- Whole cherries or olives (especially with pits)
- Raisins
- Chewing gum

Never leave an infant or young child unattended while eating. Provide small amounts of food so your child takes one bite at a time. Chop food into small pieces and peel and quarter fruits like grapes and blueberries. Also, insist that your children sit down (not run, walk, play, or lie down) while eating.

# Breakfast

# Perfect Scrambled Eggs



**To make perfect scrambled eggs you need a few basic tools and techniques, the most essential of which is using low heat. Good butter and fresh eggs from free-range chickens are also important.**

2 tablespoons unsalted butter
8 large eggs
2 tablespoons heavy cream, half-and-half, or milk
Kosher salt and freshly ground black pepper

1 Heat a 12-inch nonstick frying pan over low heat. Add the butter.

2 Break the eggs into a bowl. Add the cream, half-and-half, or milk and whisk with a fork until the yolks and whites are mixed.

3 When the butter has melted, pour the eggs into the frying pan and push the eggs around the pan with a rubber spatula so that the uncooked portions run beneath the coagulating egg. Sprinkle with salt and pepper.

4 Take the eggs off the heat before they are completely cooked, as they will continue to cook for a few seconds. Serve immediately on a warmed plate with toast.

**Serves 4**

**Variations** Add a little of one of the following combinations as the eggs finish cooking: chopped tomato and minced fresh basil; finely chopped ham and grated Swiss cheese; cottage cheese and chopped fresh chives; cream cheese, dill, and chopped lox; cooked crumbled bacon and grated cheddar cheese; chopped spinach and grated pepper Jack cheese; avocado, chopped cilantro, and salsa.

**Good to Know** Scrambled, poached, hard-boiled, soft-boiled, fried, in an omelet, a frittata, or quiche, eggs are versatile, low-cost, easy, and highly nutritious. Contrary to previous belief, new research shows that moderate consumption of eggs does not have a negative impact on cholesterol. If your child is otherwise generally eating a lowfat, low-cholesterol diet, then eggs are a good daily source of protein and essential amino acids and nutrients. But if she eats a lot of processed foods and/or cheese, then it would probably be a good idea to limit her to just a few eggs per week.

# Perfect Fried Eggs



**Eggs are a breakfast staple, and fried eggs are sure to please every individual taste. From sunny-side up to over hard, being a short-order cook isn't so hard with eggs!**

2 tablespoons unsalted butter
4 large eggs
Kosher salt and freshly ground black pepper

1 Melt the butter in a large nonstick frying pan over medium heat.

2 Crack the eggs into the pan and season with salt and pepper to taste. Let the eggs cook until the whites begin to turn opaque, 2 to 3 minutes.

3 For sunny-side-up eggs, continue cooking until the whites are set but the yolks are still runny. For over-easy, over-medium, or over-hard eggs, flip the eggs with a wide, flat spatula. Cook the over-easy eggs about 30 seconds more to set the whites; the yolks should remain runny. Cook 1½ minutes for over-medium eggs until the whites are firm and the yolks are slightly runny. Cook 2 minutes for over-hard eggs. You can pop the yolk with the spatula to make the yolk cook faster. Serve immediately.

**Serves 2**

**Good to Know** Because of the risk of salmonella, soft-boiled or runny eggs are not recommended for very young children, the elderly, and those with weakened immune systems.

## Variations

**Boiled Eggs:** Place the eggs in saucepan, cover with cold water by 2 inches, and bring to a boil over medium heat. Cover the pot, turn off the heat, and let stand 5 minutes for large, soft-boiled eggs; 10 minutes for large, medium-firm yolks; 12 to 14 minutes for large, hard-boiled eggs. Serve soft-boiled eggs in egg cups with strips of buttered toast for dipping. To peel hard-boiled eggs, immediately after cooking, transfer the eggs to an ice bath. When cooled, peel under cold running water to help separate the shells cleanly. (In general, the fresher the eggs, the harder they are to peel.)

**Poached Eggs:** Add 2 to 3 inches of water to a frying pan and bring to a boil. Add a splash of white vinegar to help the eggs hold their shape. Fresher eggs will also yield neater, round shapes. Reduce the heat to medium-low to establish a simmer. Crack each egg into a small bowl and gently ease the egg into the water. Turn off the heat, cover the pan, and let stand for 3 to 5 minutes. Remove the eggs with a slotted spoon, touch the bottom of the spoon to a towel to absorb excess water, and serve immediately.

**One-eyed Sailors:** Also called Toad in the Hole, this is a kid favorite. Use the rim of a glass to press and cut a circle out of the middle of 4 slices of bread. (You can save the circles to make French toast.) In a nonstick frying pan, heat 4 tablespoons (½ stick) unsalted butter over low heat until it is melted and the pan is hot. Place the slices of bread in the pan. Crack 4 eggs, one at a time, into a small bowl and slide each egg into the hole in each slice of bread. Cook for a few minutes until the white of the egg is firm. Then flip and cook for a couple of minutes on the opposite side until the yolk is as firm as you like. Serve with maple syrup, if desired. Serves 2 to 4.

# Classic Omelet

**A great omelet requires a hot pan. Best of all is a well-seasoned cast-iron skillet that has never seen a drop of dish detergent. Broccoli, red bell peppers, and spinach are good additions—and a bit of cheese always helps kids with veggies.**

8 large eggs
1 tablespoon whole milk, cream, or water
Kosher salt and freshly ground black pepper
2 tablespoons unsalted butter
1 cup cooked and diced meat and/or vegetables (page 55)
½ cup coarsely grated or crumbled cheese

1 In a large bowl, whisk together the eggs and milk until the yolks and whites are nice and frothy, 1 to 2 minutes. Season to taste with salt and pepper.

2 Heat a large nonstick frying pan over medium-high heat. Add the butter and swirl to coat the bottom of the pan. Heat until the butter is foaming, but do not let it brown.

3 Pour the egg mixture into the pan and let cook, undisturbed, for about 1 minute. Using a heatproof spatula, gently stir the eggs around in the pan until no raw egg is visible. Let cook a minute more or less just until set.

4 Sprinkle the meat and/or vegetables and the cheese over the top. Tilt the pan slightly to get the round sheet of egg toward one side of the pan, then use the spatula to fold the omelet in half.

5 Slide the omelet onto a plate, cut it crosswise into 4 pieces, and serve immediately.

**Serves 4**

## Variations

Try the following classic variations, or other great combinations suggested in Kitchen Sink Frittatas (page 66):

**Western:** ham, cheddar cheese, green bell peppers, onions.

**Greek:** feta cheese, olives, plum tomatoes, spinach.

**Southwestern:** salsa, avocado, corn, Monterey Jack cheese, jalapeño peppers, fresh cilantro.

**Italian:** sausage, tomatoes, garlic, fresh basil, Parmesan cheese.

**Veggie:** zucchini, tomatoes, mozzarella cheese, broccoli, mushrooms.

# Baked Eggs

**To bake, or shirr, an egg simply means to bake an egg without its shell, typically in a small ramekin. It is a convenient way to prepare and serve eggs to a crowd. If you don't have ramekins or custard cups, you can use buttered muffin tins.**

2 tablespoons unsalted butter, at room temperature
2 slices crisp, cooked bacon, crumbled
6 large eggs
3 tablespoons heavy cream
Kosher salt and freshly ground black pepper

1 Preheat the oven to 400°F. Lightly butter 6 ramekins or custard cups and place them on a baking sheet.

2 Add 1 tablespoon of the crumbled bacon to the bottom of each ramekin. Break an egg into each ramekin and drizzle 1½ teaspoons of cream over each. Season with salt and pepper to taste.

3 Bake the eggs for 10 minutes, or just until set. Serve immediately with hot, buttered toast.

**Serves 6**

## Variations

**Ham and Salsa Eggs:** Follow the preceding recipe but substitute diced ham for the bacon and add 1 tablespoon salsa to the bottom of each ramekin. Add the egg and season with salt and pepper to taste. Bake for 8 minutes, then top each egg with 1 tablespoon shredded cheddar cheese and bake for a few more minutes to melt the cheese.

**Toast and Prosciutto Eggs:** Line each buttered ramekin with 2 slices prosciutto, pressing the middle to the bottom and hanging the ends over the sides, then top with a round of lightly buttered bread cut to size. Bake for 5 minutes, then add an egg on top of the toast round in each ramekin. Bake for 10 minutes more. Sprinkle with finely grated lemon zest and minced fresh chives, if desired. Serve immediately.

# A Whirl of Smoothies



**What are smoothies made of? A cup or two of liquid, something creamy, something fruity, and a sprinkle of flavor or extra nutrients. Experiment and create your family's secret formula.**

### Berry-Oat Smoothie

2 cups milk, soy milk, or almond beverage
2 cups yogurt
2 cups frozen berries
¼ cup oat bran
½ teaspoon almond extract
6 ice cubes

### Melon-Tofu Smoothie

1 cup milk, soy milk, or almond beverage
4 ounces silken tofu
1 cup diced cantaloupe
1 nectarine, pitted
1 tablespoon honey
¼ cup freshly squeezed lemon juice
6 ice cubes

### Orange-Yogurt Smoothie

2 cups freshly squeezed orange juice
2 cups yogurt
1 banana, cut into chunks
¼ cup wheat germ
6 ice cubes

### Spinach-Banana Smoothie

2 cups milk, soy milk, or almond beverage
4 bananas, cut into chunks
2 cups chopped raw spinach
2 tablespoons ground flaxseeds
1 tablespoon honey
6 ice cubes

Combine all of the ingredients in a blender and mix until smooth. Pour into glasses and serve.

**Makes 4 to 6 servings each**





## Tips

- A protein-rich breakfast is an important start to the day because it allows the release of energy over several hours. Make sure your smoothie has protein, otherwise it will be just a big glass of sugar-spike. Some sources of protein for smoothies are milk, soy milk, almond beverage, yogurt, tofu, avocado, almond or peanut butter, or oat bran.
- Other great ingredients to keep in mind: unsweetened cocoa powder; frozen mangoes; pomegranate or cranberry juice; diced avocado; ½ cup frozen cauliflower or broccoli florets; or a handful of raw kale.
- Keep containers of cut bananas in your freezer to add to smoothies. It is a good way to use ripe bananas you did not eat in time.

**Good to Know** Flaxseeds are packed with vitamins and minerals and contain fiber, antioxidants, and omega-3 fatty acids. Because of their high-fiber content, they can have a laxative effect. A teaspoon of ground flaxseed is enough for a toddler. Buy whole flaxseeds and keep them in the refrigerator. Grind about ¼ cup at a time and use to sprinkle into shakes, granola mixes, cookie dough, or salads.

# Homemade Applesauce

**When apple season comes along, it is definitely time for applesauce. Try all the different varieties at your local farmers' market. Softer apples like McIntosh make a creamy applesauce, while hard types like Granny Smith will give you a chunkier sauce. Braeburns will make a sweet and tart sauce and Jonagolds are sweet with just a hint of tartness. Idareds make a beautiful pink sauce when cooked with their skins. Mixing varieties together will give you different flavors and textures. Red Delicious and Gala apples don't work as well cooked.**

8 medium-size apples
½ cup packed brown sugar, or granulated sugar
1 teaspoon ground cinnamon
¼ cup water, apple juice, or lemonade

1 Core and slice the apples and place them in a large nonstick pot with the remaining ingredients.

2 Cover and cook on low heat for 30 to 45 minutes, stirring every 5 minutes, until the sauce reaches the desired consistency. Cook longer for a smoother sauce.

3 Remove the skins with a fork.

4 Serve the applesauce warm or cool, any time of day, on its own, with toast or pancakes, with chicken or turkey, or with vanilla ice cream.

**Makes 6 cups**

# Blended Fruits

**A little fresh fruit purée is a wonderful thing by itself, for a little one's dessert, or on cereal in the morning. You can add or increase liquid to make smoothies.**

**Banana-Apple**

2 bananas, cut into chunks
1 cup applesauce
1 cup plain yogurt
2 tablespoons honey (optional)
4 tablespoons wheat germ for topping

**Better Than Orange Juice**

2 nectarines (or peaches), peeled, pitted, and quartered
2 cups plain yogurt
½ cup freshly squeezed orange juice
¼ cup oat bran or wheat germ
1 cup crushed ice or 1 frozen banana (optional)
¼ cup raspberries for topping

**Strawberry Frappé**

1 cup freshly squeezed grapefruit or orange juice
1 cup strawberries, hulled
3 tablespoons honey (optional)
½ cup club soda
1 cup crushed ice

**Summer Heaven**

2 papayas, peeled, seeded, and diced
1 mango, peeled, pitted, and diced
1 cup diced pineapple
2 bananas, cut into chunks
¼ cup apple juice
Juice of 1 lemon
1 cup blueberries for topping

Mix everything, except for the toppings, in a blender for 1 to 2 minutes, until smooth. Add the toppings and serve immediately.

**Makes 4 servings each**

# Fabulous Fruit!

**Ah, the scintillating strawberry, the wondrous watermelon, the to-die-for apple—even the lovely lemon. Ever available and taken for granted, fruits seldom receive adjectives like these. Well, it's time to give fruits their due. Fruits are ready-to-eat snacks in their own little edible, portable packages. Healthy in almost unlimited consumption, this food group is packed with nutrients, full of flavor, and lacking in sodium, harmful fats, and refined sugar. Even fast-food restaurants have jumped on the fruit wagon. The popularity of the smoothie has finally brought fruit into the limelight.**

NECESSARY NUTRIENTS: Maximize your intake of such goodies as carotenoids (like beta-carotene, lycopene, and lutein); phytochemical compounds (which may fight the aging process); folate, potassium, and of course, copious amounts of vitamins C, A, and E, among others. Guava, watermelon, kiwi, papaya, berries, and grapefruit are among the highest scorers in overall nutrition. It's easy to snack on the recommended amounts of fruit, generally from 2 to 2.5 cups per day, or 4 or 5 servings. Have a smoothie or an apple with peanut butter.

NO SUCH THING AS A BAD FRUIT: In general, even people who eat fruit that has pesticide residue (see Buying Organic, page 248) have a lower risk of disease than people who don't eat enough fruit. High in water and fiber, fresh fruit delivers everything good without all the calories. Substituting fruits for higher-calorie foods assists with weight loss. Further, the unusually high potassium content of fruits, especially bananas and oranges, has been shown to dramatically lower blood pressure, stave off vascular damage, and improve heart function. Other compounds in fruits, like blueberries, have helped rats find their way through mazes, and may even lower the risk of cognitive decline.

**DECORATIVE AND DELICIOUS:** Turn a meal into a fiesta of colors and shapes with fruit. The amazing variety of reds, blues, purples, yellows, and greens is visually tantalizing and tempting. And think of the range of textures and tastes: the creaminess of an avocado, the crunchiness of an apple, the way a squeeze of lemon is a natural salt substitute.

**WHAT YOU MUST KNOW:** Thick-rinded fruits like melons, pineapple, kiwi, and grapefruit, while low in pesticide residue, carry the greatest risk of infection from harmful long-living bacteria. It's easy for the outside of a fruit to become contaminated from soil or water, and since we don't eat it, we generally don't worry about the thick, hard-to-wash skin. Tragically, in 2011, listeria on cantaloupe killed at least fifteen people in the United States. Although sanitation and food prep is key, many grocers reported being unaware of precautions to insure produce safety. Knives used for slicing will carry organisms on the outsides of rinds to the insides of the fruits. Cantaloupes are safe to eat, but you should scrub these and other thick-rinded produce, including cucumbers and grapefruit, very well with a brush. Consume as soon as possible after slicing; this way, microbes aren't given the chance to grow. It goes without saying that buying prepackaged cantaloupe sliced at a chain store is risky. Likewise, it's not a good idea to submerge that twist of lemon in your drink unless you know it's been properly washed.

# Kitchen Sink Frittatas

**The name we gave to our version of the classic Italian open-egg omelet refers to the fact that you can throw pretty much any ingredient into it and it will be delicious. A frittata is the perfect way to use up the bits and pieces from last night's supper, and is one of our favorite uses for leftover spaghetti.**

10 large eggs
1 cup favorite shredded or crumbled cheese
Kosher salt and freshly ground black pepper
1 tablespoon olive oil
1 to 2 cups leftover cooked vegetables, meat, pasta, or whatever you have on hand, or see page 67 for ideas

1 Preheat the oven to 425°F.

2 In a large bowl, whisk the eggs and cheese together and season with salt and pepper to taste.

3 Heat the oil in a 10-inch ovenproof nonstick frying pan over medium heat. Add the leftover ingredients and cook a few minutes, stirring, to heat through.

4 Reduce the heat to medium-low. Add the egg mixture and cook, stirring gently, until the eggs begin to set. Continue to cook the eggs, undisturbed, until they begin to set around the edges, 2 to 3 minutes more.

5 Transfer the skillet to the oven and bake until the eggs are just firm in the center, about 5 minutes more.

6 Let the frittata cool slightly, then cut it into wedges and serve directly from the pan.

**Serves 4 to 6**

**Variations** Try creating your own frittatas, using the combinations listed for variations of the Classic Omelet (page 54), or try these great suggestions:

- Sautéed mushrooms, thyme, and fontina cheese.
- Blanched asparagus and fresh goat cheese.
- Sautéed spinach, crumbled bacon, and cheddar cheese.
- Roasted bell peppers, sautéed onions, Italian sausage, and marinara sauce.
- Sliced prosciutto, fresh mozzarella cheese, and halved cherry tomatoes.
- Cooked shredded chicken, roasted corn kernels, and minced fresh herbs.
- See also Spinach and Potato Frittata (page 83).

## Tip

**Make it a Quiche:** Add a little dairy to your egg mixture (milk, half-and-half, or heavy cream) and a crust and you have a quiche! See Mini Ham and Pea Quiches (page 173) for more ideas and tips on freezing your fritatta or quiches.

# Cinnamon Toast

**Well, we thought we would put this in the breakfast chapter because it had to go somewhere. But it could just as easily have been put in the snacks or desserts chapters. Warm, simple, and comforting, cinnamon toast was always the treat of choice in Natasha's childhood, made with Honey Whole Wheat Momma Bread (page 94). Our friend Maren is from Minnesota—land of cold winters—and the milk-toast variation comes from her childhood.**

2 pieces warm, buttered toast
1½ teaspoons ground cinnamon
1½ tablespoons granulated sugar

1 While the bread is toasting, combine the cinnamon and sugar in a small bowl and mix well.

2 Butter the toast and then immediately spoon the cinnamon sugar over the melting butter. Serve immediately.

**Serves 1**

## Variation

**Cinnamon Milk Toast:** Cut the warm cinnamon toast into bite-size pieces and place in a shallow bowl. Pour ½ cup warm milk over the toast. Eat with a spoon before the bread becomes too soggy!

Bond Bread

# A Pancake of Your Own



**Using a spoon or poultry baster, dribble a bit of batter in the shape of your child's initial—writing it backwards—onto the pan a few seconds before you spoon a circle of pancake batter over it. When you flip the pancake, the initial will appear on the other side inside the circular pancake. You can also make outlines of animals, dollar signs, or heart shapes using this same method.**

1½ cups unbleached white flour
1 tablespoon sugar
¾ teaspoon kosher salt
1 tablespoon baking powder
3 large eggs, separated
4 tablespoons (½ stick) unsalted butter, melted, plus more for frying
2 cups whole milk

1. Preheat the oven to 200°F and put a plate into it to warm.
2. In a large bowl, combine the dry ingredients. In a separate bowl, beat the egg yolks with the melted butter and milk. Stir the wet mixture into the dry mixture. In a third bowl, beat the egg whites until they are fluffy and fold them into the batter.
3. Place a frying pan over medium-high heat, add some butter, and swirl to coat the bottom of the pan. Dribble your backwards initial or shape onto the pan first. Then drop a large spoonful of batter on top of the browning initial. When the top of the pancake is covered in small bubbles, flip the pancake and brown the opposite side.
4. Transfer the pancakes, as you make them, to the plate in the oven to keep warm until ready to serve.
5. Serve the pancakes with your favorite toppings—applesauce, maple syrup, lemon juice, and confectioners' sugar, or your favorite jam.

**Serves 4 to 6**

# Whole Wheat Buttermilk Pancakes

**Buttermilk is a fermented milk product with a nutritional profile similar to regular milk, and does not actually contain butter! It is the magic ingredient for flavorful, light, and fluffy pancakes.**

2 cups buttermilk
2 large eggs, at room temperature
6 tablespoons unsalted butter, melted
¾ cup all-purpose flour
1 teaspoon kosher salt
2 teaspoons baking soda

1 In a medium bowl, whisk together the buttermilk, eggs, and melted butter.

2 In a small bowl, stir together the flour, salt, and baking soda until well blended, then stir them into the buttermilk mixture just until blended. Do not overmix. A few lumps or traces of flour are okay.

3 Heat a large nonstick frying pan, cast-iron skillet, or pancake griddle until medium hot. Grease it with a light coating of butter.

4 Spoon out about 3 tablespoons of batter per pancake. Immediately spread out the batter with the back of a spoon so the pancakes are not too thick.

5 When a few bubbles break on top, flip each pancake over and cook briefly on the opposite side until the pancake is slightly puffed up and lightly browned. Serve immediately with real maple syrup.

**Serves 4 to 6**

# Swedish Pancakes

**We cannot have pancakes in the book without the pancakes that Lena, Natasha's mom, grew up with in Sweden. They are thinner than American pancakes, more like crêpes, and undeniably delicious. It is easier to make them if your frying pan has a good heavy bottom; this evens out the heat. You can serve these with lingonberries, as Lena does, or shaved chocolate and confectioners' sugar, or lemon juice and a sprinkle of granulated sugar. If you smear them with apricot jam, add a dollop of whipped cream, and roll them up, they make a pretty perfect dessert as well.**

⅓ cup sugar
1⅓ cups all-purpose flour
4 large whole eggs
2 large egg yolks
2¼ cups whole milk
8 tablespoons (1 stick) unsalted butter, melted, plus more as needed

1 In a bowl, sift together the sugar and flour. In a separate bowl, beat together the eggs and milk. Add to the dry ingredients, then add the melted butter. Let the batter rest for about 30 minutes, if possible.

2 On a hot pancake griddle or in a large, heavy-bottomed frying pan, about 10 inches in diameter, melt a bit of butter over medium-high heat. Pour about ¼ cup of the batter into the pan and swirl the pan around until the batter forms a large, thin circle. Quickly brown; this will take less than 1 minute. Flip the pancake over and brown on the opposite side. Transfer the pancake to a warm plate in the oven.

3 Repeat the procedure with the remaining batter, adding more butter to the pan as needed. Serve warm with the accompaniment of your choice.

**Serves 4 to 6**

# Whole Wheat Banana Nut Waffles

**These waffles are a snap to throw together and they pack a lot of nutritional goodness. Make a big batch and freeze leftover waffles for later in the week. They will reheat to crispy perfection in the toaster oven in minutes, and they taste better than any store-bought frozen waffles.**

2 large egg yolks
2 cups whole milk
2 cups whole wheat flour
1 tablespoon baking powder
¼ teaspoon kosher salt
⅓ cup canola oil
2 bananas, mashed
½ cup walnuts, chopped
2 large egg whites, stiffly beaten
2 tablespoons butter, melted

1. Preheat a waffle iron.
2. In a large bowl, whisk together all of the ingredients, except for the egg whites and butter, until combined and the batter is smooth. Using a rubber or silicone spatula, gently fold in the beaten egg whites.
3. Brush a bit of butter on the top and bottom plates of the waffle iron. Pour approximately ½ cup of batter onto the preheated waffle iron. Close and cook until golden. Repeat with the remaining batter. Serve warm.

**Makes eight 8-inch waffles**

## Variations

**Chocolate Nut Butter Waffles:** Instead of the banana and walnuts, fold 1 cup chocolate chips into the waffle batter and cook as directed. Spread the hot waffles with peanut or almond butter and drizzle the tops with honey. Serve warm.

**Bacon and Cheese Waffles:** Eliminate the bananas and walnuts. Fry 8 strips bacon and crumble. Grate ½ cup cheddar cheese and fold into the batter. Pour ½ cup of batter onto the preheated waffle maker and sprinkle a bit of bacon on top. Cook as directed. Serve warm.

# Great Granola



**This is a recipe Natasha's family has been using for decades. It hails from an old family friend on the West Coast. The powdered milk helps with binding and also raises the protein content. If you do a lot of camping, be sure to take some of this along. You just add water and—voila!—granola cereal and milk!**

5 cups rolled oats
1 cup wheat germ
1 cup low-fat powdered milk
1 cup chopped nuts (e.g. almond, macadamia, filbert, Brazil)
1 cup sunflower seeds
1 cup pumpkin seeds
1 cup shredded coconut
1½ cups canola oil
1½ cups honey (or a combination of honey and maple syrup)
2 cups raisins
2 cups dried apricots, chopped

1. Preheat the oven to 300°F.
2. Combine all of the ingredients, except the raisins and apricots, and spread out onto parchment paper–lined baking sheets. The more sheets you use the faster it will cook.
3. Bake for 45 minutes to 1 hour, stirring occasionally. You can vary the cooking time so it's crunchier or softer, depending on what you like.
4. Reduce the oven temperature to 250°F and mix in the raisins and dried apricots. Bake for another 30 minutes. Cool completely before serving or storing in an airtight container.

**Makes about 4 quarts**

**Variations** Also try these simple combinations: Just preheat the oven to 300°F and bake on baking sheets for 30 to 35 minutes, stirring halfway through the baking time.

**Oatmeal Raisin Granola:** 2 cups rolled oats, 2 tablespoons canola oil, ¼ cup honey, 1 teaspoon molasses, 2 tablespoons raisins, ½ teaspoon ground cinnamon, ½ teaspoon pumpkin-pie spice.

**Chocolaty Goodness Granola:** 2 cups rolled oats, 2 tablespoons canola oil, ¼ cup honey, 2 tablespoons unsweetened cocoa powder. After baking and cooling, add 2 tablespoons dark-chocolate chips.

**Makes 8 servings each**

**Tip** For extra nutrition, add 2 tablespoons ground chia seeds or ground flaxseeds to your mix.

# Hot Cereal

**Whole grains are excellent sources of nutrition and fiber, and old-fashioned hot cereal is a great breakfast standard. The following hot-cereal chart will hopefully inspire you and your children to reach less often for a bowl of sugary cold cereal. An easy way to avoid adding sugar at the table is by tossing a quarter cup of raisins into the cereal while it's cooking—their flavor will sweeten the cereal and the raisins will become nice and plump for extra-chewy porridge goodness.**

1 Bring water to a boil.

2 Add grains or cereal. (If using milk, add grains to cold milk and bring to a boil together.)

3 Simmer partially covered for the time indicated in the following chart, or prepare as directed on the package.

## Variations

- Flavor with a teaspoon of vanilla extract, almond extract, cinnamon, or orange zest.
- Top it off with fresh fruit, such as peaches, apples, pears, berries, or banana slices; or dried fruits, such as cranberries, raisins, dates, or dried-fruit slices; or applesauce.
- Give it some crunch with walnuts, sliced almonds, sesame seeds, wheat germ, pecans, or chopped hazelnuts.
- Stir in a spoonful of honey, maple syrup, brown sugar, marmalade, fruit spread or jam, or molasses.

## Grain Preparation Chart

| GRAIN | Cups of Grain (dry) | Cups of Water/Milk | Minutes to Simmer | Yield in Cups |
|---|---|---|---|---|
| barley, pearl | 1 | 2–2½ | 15 | 3 |
| brown rice | 1 | 2 | 45 | 3 |
| buckwheat groats (kasha) | 1 | 2 | 15–20 | 2½ |
| bulgur | 1 | 2 | 15 | 2½ |
| cream of wheat | ½ | 2 | ½ | 2 |
| millet | 1 | 3 | 45 | 3 |
| quick oats | 1 | 2 | 1 | 2 |
| quinoa | 1 | 2 | 15 | 2 |
| rolled oats | 1 | 2 | 15 | 2 |

**Good to Know** More and more studies show that whole grains and other unprocessed carbohydrates can improve health in many ways. Whole grains:

- reduce the risk of cardiovascular disease
- offer protection against some forms of cancer
- aid in preventing type 2 diabetes
- help prevent constipation
- help you to live longer

# Overnight Oatmeal

**We love steel-cut oats—the texture and flavor are much more interesting than rolled oats. Steel-cut oatmeal takes quite a bit longer to cook than rolled oats, but you can get around this by starting the oatmeal the night before.**

- 1 cup steel-cut oats
- 1 teaspoon kosher salt
- ½ cup golden raisins
- ½ cup dried cherries or cranberries
- ½ cup chopped pecans

1 The night before you plan to eat the oatmeal, pour 4 cups of water into a 2-quart saucepan. Add the steel-cut oats, salt, dried fruit, and pecans. Bring the oatmeal to a boil. Turn off the heat, cover, and let sit overnight.

2 In the morning, heat the oatmeal and simmer until tender, about 20 minutes. Leftover oatmeal can be refrigerated and reheated for several days.

**Serves 4**

## Variation

**Slow Cooker Oatmeal:** Add steel-cut oats and liquid (water, milk, or a combination) in a 1:4 ratio in a slow cooker, leaving 2 inches of space at the top. Add a pinch of ground cinnamon and salt, and some dried fruit. Stir, cover, and cook on low for 8 to 9 hours.

**Glazed Oatmeal:** Put a serving of cooked oatmeal into a shallow soup bowl. Arrange thinly sliced fruit over the top of the oatmeal in a single layer. Sprinkle evenly with superfine sugar and run under a very hot broiler until the top is caramelized.

# Home Fries

**Potatoes don't deserve their bad rap. They are a good source of dietary energy and some micronutrients, and a potato's protein content is very high in comparison with other roots and tubers. Potatoes are low in fat—if you don't drown them in sour cream and cheese or deep-fry them in oil! Enjoy them as part of a balanced diet with plenty of other vegetables and whole grain foods.**

2 pounds small red potatoes
Kosher salt and freshly ground black pepper
¼ cup canola oil
1 small to medium yellow onion, peeled and sliced

1. Scrub the potatoes, place them in a saucepan, and cover with cold water. Bring to a boil, lower the heat, and simmer, uncovered, until the potatoes are soft but not fully cooked, about 15 minutes. Drain and cool.
2. When the potatoes are cool, cut them into ¼-inch-thick slices. Season with salt and pepper to taste.
3. Heat the oil in a large cast-iron skillet until hot. Add the potatoes and begin frying on one side over medium-high heat. After several minutes, add the onion. When the bottoms of the potatoes are golden brown, turn and fry the opposite sides, 10 to 12 minutes total. The potatoes should be slightly crisp on the outside and soft on the inside.
4. Using a slotted spoon, transfer the home fries to paper towels to drain excess oil, then serve.

**Serves 4 to 6**

## Variation

**Spinach and Potato Frittata:** Plan ahead for another meal and cook up a few extra potatoes in Step 1 and refrigerate. To make the frittata, slice the potatoes. Heat 2 tablespoons olive oil in a medium cast-iron skillet over medium heat. Add the sliced potatoes to the skillet. Mix in 1 cup torn fresh spinach leaves, 2 tablespoons scallions, and a minced garlic clove. Season with salt and pepper to taste. Cook 1 to 2 minutes until the spinach is wilted. In a medium bowl, beat together 6 large eggs and ⅓ cup whole milk. Pour the mixture into the skillet over the vegetables and sprinkle with ¼ cup shredded cheddar cheese. Reduce the heat to low, cover, and cook 5 to 7 minutes, until the eggs are set. Serves 6.

**Tip** Sweet potatoes have a higher nutritional value than white potatoes. They contain beta-carotene and are high in fiber, folate, potassium, and other vitamins. Try sweet potatoes instead of white potatoes in your recipes—just increase your cooking time slightly. See also Tip on page 303.

# Heavenly Hash Browns

**Bacon—we can take it or leave it, but there's nothing better with eggs in the morning than hash browns. If you find yourself with a giant bag of potatoes and don't have a basement for storage, try freezing shredded potatoes to use in hash-brown casseroles (see Variation, page 85).**

2 large unpeeled baking potatoes
2 tablespoons unsalted butter
Kosher salt and freshly ground black pepper

1. Scrub the potatoes and grate them through the large holes of a box grater, skin and all.
2. Put the butter in a large cast-iron skillet and melt over medium-high heat.
3. Add the potatoes to the skillet, spreading them out evenly and patting them down with a spatula. Sprinkle the tops generously with salt and pepper.
4. Fry the potatoes until they are brown and crispy on the bottom, 5 to 8 minutes.
5. Flip the potatoes, in sections if necessary, and fry for another 5 minutes, or until brown and crispy on the opposite side. Serve the hash browns hot with ketchup or salsa.

**Serves 4**

## Variation

**Ham and Hash Brown Casserole:** Preheat the oven to 375°F. Lightly oil a 13 x 9-inch pan. Heat 3 tablespoons canola oil in a large cast-iron skillet over medium heat. Add 2 pounds shredded potatoes, ½ cup chopped onions, and 1 cup chopped red bell peppers. Cook until the potatoes begin to brown, about 10 minutes. Spread the potato mixture over the bottom of the prepared pan. Top with 1 cup cubed ham or leftover chicken or sausage. In a large bowl, beat 10 large eggs and season with salt and pepper. Pour the eggs over the potatoes in the pan. Gently stir to coat all of the ingredients with the beaten eggs. Sprinkle with ½ cup shredded cheddar cheese. Bake, covered with aluminum foil, for 25 minutes. Remove the foil and bake for 5 minutes more. Serves 8.

**Tip** To freeze shredded potatoes, grate the potatoes and place them in a bowl of cold water to prevent oxidation until all of the potatoes have been shredded. Drain and blanch the shredded potatoes in boiling water for about 3 minutes. Drain again, rinse under cold running water, drain a third time, and pat dry. Pack the potatoes into freezer containers or resealable freezer bags. Use directly from the freezer in favorite dishes calling for frozen hash-brown potatoes.

# Blueberry Peach Breakfast Parfait



**The possibilities for fruity breakfast parfaits are endless, but here is a scrumptious concoction and a variation to inspire you. Greek-style yogurt is now readily available in supermarkets. Its live and active culture content is a good deal higher than that of normal yogurt, so choose it when you can.**

2 cups fresh blueberries
½ cup peach jam
2 cups plain Greek-style yogurt
½ cup sliced almonds, toasted

1 In a microwave-safe bowl, combine the blueberries and jam. Microwave on high power for 2 to 3 minutes, until the berries are soft. Cool to room temperature.

2 In four sundae glasses, layer a few tablespoons of yogurt, a few tablespoons of blueberry sauce, and a sprinkling of toasted almonds. Repeat to make two to three more layers. Chill the parfaits until ready to serve.

**Serves 4**

## Variation

**Choco-Berry Crunch Parfait:** In a small bowl, gently mix 2 cups fresh raspberries with 1 tablespoon sugar. In a separate bowl, combine 2 cups plain Greek-style yogurt with 2 tablespoons unsweetened cocoa powder. In 4 sundae glasses, add a few tablespoons of the yogurt mixture, followed by a few tablespoons of raspberries. Sprinkle a layer of granola on top; you will need about ½ cup total. Repeat to make three more layers. Chill the parfaits until ready to serve. Serves 4.

# Breakfast Burritos

**Burritos are fun and easy to create for any meal with ingredients on hand. These burritos make a great to-go, energy-packed breakfast when the kids are off to early soccer practice. Just wrap the burritos in aluminum foil to keep them warm—and don't forget the napkins.**

1 tablespoon unsalted butter
1 potato, quartered and sliced
½ onion, chopped
4 large eggs, beaten
4 ounces cooked turkey sausage or other favorite precooked sausage, sliced
4 ounces grated cheddar cheese
Four 9-inch whole wheat tortillas
Hot pepper sauce

1 Melt the butter in a nonstick frying pan over medium-high heat. Add the sliced potatoes and chopped onion and fry, turning frequently, until brown and cooked through.

2 Stir in the beaten eggs and sliced turkey sausage. Cook until the eggs are to the desired consistency.

3 Sprinkle the grated cheese on top and allow it to melt.

4 Place a serving of the scrambled mixture in the center of each tortilla, add hot pepper sauce to taste, and wrap each tortilla. Wrap each burrito well in aluminum foil and serve.

**Serves 4**

## Variation

**Baked Beans Burrito:** Try baked beans in your burrito. Melt 1 tablespoon unsalted butter in a frying pan over medium-high heat, add ¼ cup chopped onion, and cook until golden. Add one 15-ounce can baked beans and bring to a simmer. Remove from the heat and set aside. In a separate frying pan, fry 4 large eggs (Perfect Fried Eggs, page 52). Divide the beans and eggs among four 9-inch whole wheat tortillas and top with grated cheddar cheese. The baked beans can also be served simply with eggs and whole wheat toast. Serves 4.

# Banana Oatmeal Muffins

**This low-fat, high-fiber muffin is a great alternative to its less healthy white-flour counterparts. The banana and yogurt make these muffins moist and satisfying.**

1 cup old-fashioned rolled oats
1 cup whole wheat flour
¼ cup packed brown sugar
1 teaspoon baking powder
½ teaspoon baking soda
½ teaspoon ground cinnamon
¼ teaspoon freshly grated nutmeg
2 large eggs
2 tablespoons vegetable oil
2 ripe bananas, mashed
1 cup raisins, fresh or frozen blueberries, strawberries, or raspberries (optional)
1 cup plain yogurt

1 Preheat the oven to 400°F. Line the wells of a standard 12-cup muffin pan with paper liners, or grease them lightly with butter.

2 Grind the rolled oats in a food processor, or crush them in a plastic bag using a rolling pin.

3 In a large bowl, mix the crushed, rolled oats together with the flour, sugar, baking powder, baking soda, cinnamon, and nutmeg.

4 In a separate bowl, mix together the eggs, oil, bananas, fruit, if using, and the yogurt.

5 Fold the wet mixture into the dry ingredients until just combined; do not overmix.

6 Spoon the batter into the prepared muffin pan and bake for 20 to 25 minutes.

**Makes 12 muffins**

# Baked Apples Stuffed with Granola

**In the fall, a delicious, raw, crisp apple can't be beat. But after a few weeks of apple season, the family might like some variation. Try something warm, sweet, and tender on a cool morning. Served with yogurt, these stuffed apples are a complete breakfast.**

- 4 large apples (tarter varieties work best)
- ⅔ cup favorite granola with nuts, or Great Granola (page 76)
- ⅓ cup wheat germ
- 2 tablespoons honey or brown sugar
- ½ cup apple juice or cider
- Plain yogurt

1. Preheat the oven to 375°F.
2. Core the apples using a paring knife, removing a cone shape out of the apples' centers; wide at the stem and tapering down. Use an apple corer or spoon to help scoop out the center. Set the cored apples in a 9-inch pie plate.
3. Mix together the granola, wheat germ, and honey or sugar. Stuff the centers of the apples with the mixture until full, piling the extra mixture on top.
4. Pour the juice into the bottom of the pie plate. Cover the plate with aluminum foil and bake for 30 to 45 minutes. Test the apples for tenderness and bake longer, if desired; the apples should be soft but not mushy, and easily cut with a table knife.
5. Let cool 5 minutes and serve with yogurt. These baked apples are also delicious served with vanilla ice cream as a dessert.

**Serves 4**

# Honey Whole Wheat Momma Bread

**Natasha has made this bread with her mother and sister for Thanksgiving for more than twenty-five years. They make enough to freeze, give away, and eat for breakfast with butter and honey. On the day after Thanksgiving, they use it to make sandwiches with leftover stuffing, turkey, lingonberries, and gravy.**

1 tablespoon sugar
4 cups lukewarm water
3 packages active dry yeast
1½ cups (3 sticks) unsalted butter, melted
3 tablespoons kosher salt
½ cup honey
⅓ to ½ cup molasses
5 large eggs, at room temperature
3 pounds (9 cups) whole wheat flour
2 pounds (6 cups) unbleached white flour

1. In a large bowl, combine the sugar with 2 cups of the lukewarm water. Add the yeast. Set aside in a warmish place for 15 to 20 minutes until proofed and foamy.
2. In the following order, and mixing as you go, add the butter, salt, honey, molasses, eggs, and the remaining 2 cups lukewarm water. Gradually mix in the whole wheat flour, a cup at a time.
3. Reserve about a cup of the white flour for kneading. Gradually add the remaining white flour, continuing to mix. Let the dough rest for 10 minutes.
4. Transfer the dough to a lightly floured work surface and knead for at least 10 to 15 minutes. If the dough is sticky, sprinkle it lightly with a little more white flour as you work.

5 Butter a large bowl. Turn the dough in the bowl to coat with the butter. Cover the dough loosely with a warm, damp dish towel and set aside in a warmish place to rise for 1⅓ to 2 hours. Punch it down and let it rise again for 30 minutes or so.

6 Preheat the oven to 400°F. Butter five 9 x 5 x 3-inch loaf pans or 2 baking sheets.

7 Transfer the dough to a lightly floured work surface. Cut into 5 pieces. Knead each piece, shaping it into a loaf. Press the loaves into the prepared pans or place them on the baking sheets. Cover again and let rise for 30 minutes.

8 Bake all the loaves together for 10 minutes. Reduce the oven temperature to 350°F. Bake until the bread is golden brown, about another 30 minutes. Remove the loaves from the pans and transfer to wire racks to cool slightly. Serve the warm bread with butter and thick honey.

**Makes 5 loaves**

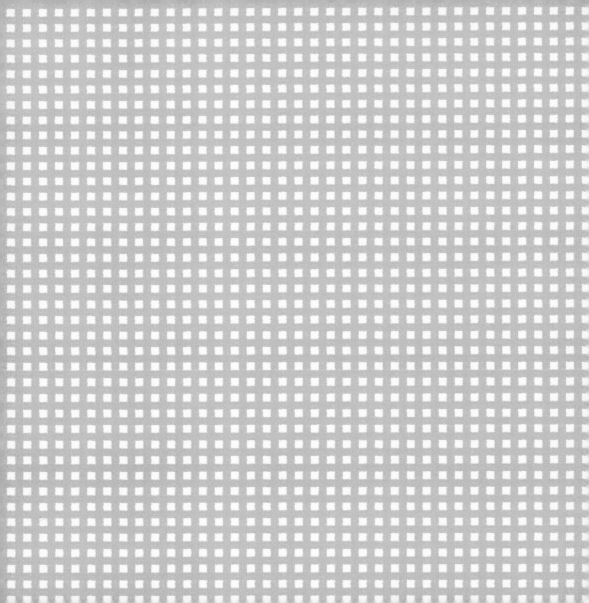

# Soups & Sandwiches

# Basic Chicken Stock

**Sometimes it seems like every recipe calls for chicken stock and we go through batches like water. You can get away with the low-sodium packaged or canned broth in most cases when a recipe calls for just a cup, but nothing beats homemade stock in soups. Make batches of this stock on weekends and freeze in containers. You will be eternally grateful to find it in your freezer when sore throat and flu season strikes. Freezing some of the stock in ice cube trays is also a good idea for those times when you need a small amount. Just transfer the frozen cubes when solid to plastic freezer bags for storage.**

3 to 4 pounds chicken parts
½ cup each diced carrot, onion, and celery
Bouquet garni (a few parsley stems and sprigs of thyme, a bay leaf, and 5 whole black peppercorns wrapped in a cheesecloth square and tied)

1 Put the chicken into a large stockpot, cover with cold water by several inches, and set over medium heat. Bring just to a boil and quickly lower the heat to a simmer. Skim off the scum that rises to the surface and continue skimming until it is no longer produced. Be diligent about skimming so that the scum is not incorporated into the stock, and the finished broth is clear and not cloudy.

2 Add the diced vegetables and the bouquet garni. Simmer, uncovered, for 4 hours.

3 Cool down the stock quickly. Strain and transfer to containers. Refrigerate for up to 4 days or freeze for up to 6 months.

**Makes 3 to 4 quarts**

## Variations

**Enhanced Stock:** If you don't have the energy or time to make homemade broth regularly, try enhancing store-bought stock. To a medium pot add 4 cups low-sodium, store-bought chicken broth, 1 roughly chopped carrot, 1 small roughly chopped onion, 1 garlic clove, and a few peppercorns, and bring just to a boil. Lower the heat and simmer, uncovered, for 10 to 20 minutes. Strain and season with salt and pepper to taste. Makes 4 cups.

**Asian-style Stock:** Use this as a base for Asian noodle soups. To a medium pot, add 4 cups chicken or vegetable stock, 2 tablespoons soy sauce, 2 sliced scallions, and 2 thin slices peeled fresh ginger, and bring just to a boil. Lower the heat and simmer, uncovered, for 10 to 20 minutes. Strain and season with pepper to taste. Makes 4 cups.

**Herbed Stock with Pasta:** Here is a little something to hit the spot. To a medium pot, add 4 cups chicken stock (homemade is best here) and 2 sprigs rosemary or 1 bunch thyme and bring just to a boil. Lower the heat and simmer, uncovered, for 10 to 15 minutes. Strain and season with salt and pepper to taste. Add a little cooked rice or orzo pasta or small cheese tortellini. Serves 4.

# Basic Vegetable Stock

**To make a basic vegetable stock, just cook a bunch of vegetables and herbs in a pot with a little oil for 30 minutes to release their juices, then add water and simmer for 45 minutes. For a large batch of stock, which requires more vegetables, it is easier to roast the vegetables in the oven first. The roasting will also add a bit of caramelized flavor and depth to your stock.**

1 pound yellow onions, peeled and roughly chopped
1 pound carrots, roughly chopped
2- to 3-pound mix of other vegetables (tomatoes, green bell peppers, turnips, fennel, leeks, etc.), roughly chopped
2 tablespoons olive oil
6 garlic cloves, peeled
6 whole black peppercorns
1 pound celery, roughly chopped
1 bunch flat-leaf parsley, chopped

1 Preheat the oven to 450°F. On a baking sheet, toss the onion, carrot, and vegetable mix with the olive oil and roast the vegetables in the oven, stirring every 15 minutes, for about 1 hour until browned and the onions have started to caramelize.

2 In a large stockpot, combine the roasted vegetables, garlic, peppercorns, celery, and parsley with 4 quarts water. Bring to a boil, lower the heat, and simmer, uncovered, until the liquid has reduced by half.

3 Cool down the stock quickly. Strain and transfer to containers. Refrigerate for up to 4 days or freeze for up to 6 months.

**Makes 2 quarts**

**Ideas** Here are some quick soup ideas using homemade chicken or vegetable stock. With the delicious foundation of homemade stock, all you need are a few additional ingredients to add variety or more substance.

**Easy Chicken Noodle Soup:** Gently simmer 6 cups homemade chicken broth with 1 boneless, skinless chicken breast for about 15 minutes, until cooked through. Remove the chicken, let cool, and shred. Add one 10-ounce bag frozen cut vegetables (peas, carrots, broccoli, etc.) and simmer until heated through, about 5 minutes. Add the shredded chicken and 1 to 2 cups cooked noodles. Serves 4 to 6.

**Quick Bean Soup:** Simmer 5 cups homemade chicken or vegetable stock with two 15-ounce cans cannellini or other white beans, rinsed and drained, and 4 crushed garlic cloves for 20 minutes. Stir in one 12-ounce bag fresh spinach. Serve the soup drizzled with a bit of olive oil and sprinkled with grated Parmesan cheese. Serves 4 to 6.

**Summer Vegetable and Pesto Soup:** Simmer 5 cups homemade chicken or vegetable stock with ½ cup each diced green beans, zucchini, and tomato for 8 minutes, or until the vegetables are tender. Stir in ½ cup cooked cannellini or kidney beans and 1 cup Pesto Sauce (page 252). Serves 4 to 6.

**Asian Noodle Soup:** Simmer 6 cups Asian-style Stock (page 99) with 1 cup tofu pieces or sliced chicken for about 5 minutes. Add 2 cups sliced bok choy or kale and simmer until the vegetables are tender, about 5 minutes. Add 4 ounces rice vermicelli or udon noodles and cook a few minutes more, until tender or heated through. Serve the soup in bowls, garnished with a handful of bean sprouts or chopped fresh cilantro and a wedge of lime. Serves 4 to 6.

# Mixed Vegetable Soup

**This easy soup has virtues well beyond the nutrients it contains. First, you can make it with any combination of vegetables you have on hand, although onions and carrots are essential. Second, it can be made without meat of any kind. Lastly, it improves as it sits in the refrigerator, should you choose not to eat the whole pot of it on the first day.**

- 2 tablespoons olive or canola oil
- 2 medium onions, chopped
- 3 carrots, peeled and diced
- 1 celery stalk, with leaves, diced
- 1 leek, well washed, white and pale green parts only, sliced
- 4 cups mixed diced vegetables, such as peeled turnips, potatoes, mushrooms, bell peppers, zucchini, green beans, sliced cabbage, tomatoes, or corn kernels
- 1 cup chopped greens, such as spinach, kale, arugula, Swiss chard, or cabbage (optional)
- 8 cups vegetable broth, or chicken or beef stock
- 1 bay leaf
- One 15-ounce can chickpeas or cannellini beans, rinsed and drained
- Kosher salt and freshly ground black pepper
- Grated Parmesan cheese (optional)

1 Heat the oil in a large pot over medium heat. Add the onions, carrots, celery, and leek and sauté until soft, about 10 minutes.

2 Add the mixed vegetables, the greens, if using, the broth, and the bay leaf. Simmer for 45 minutes, or until all the vegetables are tender. Add the canned beans, and simmer for another 20 minutes. If the soup gets too thick, add a bit of water until it

reaches the consistency you prefer. Season with salt and pepper to taste and remove and discard the bay leaf.

3 Ladle the soup into deep bowls, sprinkle the grated Parmesan over the top, if you like, and serve.

**Serves 6 to 8**

## Tip

**Slow Cooker Soups:** A slow cooker is a great tool in every busy mom's kitchen. Alice sometimes put on a 10-hour soup overnight to have lunch ready for the next day. Or a 4-hour soup is a convenient option to put on before you go to the park with the kids—you don't have to worry about hurrying home because the soup is on the stovetop. This soup and your other favorite soup recipes can be easily adapted for the slow cooker. Browning adds flavor but is not essential (except for ground meat to reduce risk of contamination). Use half to three-quarters of the liquid called for. A soup that cooks for 1½ to 2 hours on the stovetop will likely take about 4 hours on the low setting in a slow cooker. Add milk, cheese, other dairy products, and canned beans during the last hour of cooking, or stir in at the end.

# Puréed Vegetable Soups

**Get your veggies in puréed, creamy soups—this is a delicious way to eat your colors (see page 258). This master recipe will start you on your way to numerous combinations and flavors. Try some of the simple favorites suggested in the Variations and experiment to create your own. For puréed soups with more of a twist in steps and flavorings, see the following pages.**

1¼ cups minced, finely chopped, or thinly sliced aromatics (onions, shallots, carrots, celery, leeks, garlic, or fresh ginger)
1 to 2 tablespoons unsalted butter or olive oil
Kosher salt and freshly ground black pepper
1½ pounds vegetables, sliced or diced
5 cups chicken or vegetable stock
¼ cup cream, buttermilk, or Greek-style yogurt (optional)
½ to 1½ teaspoons lemon or lime juice, or vinegar (red, white, apple cider, rice, or balsamic vinegar) (optional)

1. In a large pot, sauté the aromatics in the butter with a pinch of salt over medium-low heat until soft, 8 to 10 minutes.
2. Add the vegetables and stock, bring to a boil, lower the heat to medium, and simmer, uncovered, until the vegetables are very tender, 10 to 20 minutes, depending on the vegetables.
3. Let the soup cool for 5 minutes. Using an immersion blender, a regular blender, or a food processor, carefully purée the soup until smooth. Return the soup to the pot.

4 Season with salt and pepper to taste, and whisk in the dairy for a creamier consistency, if using. Add a little lemon or lime juice, or vinegar for a touch of brightness, if desired. Serve immediately.

**Serves 4 to 6**

## Variations

**Tomato Soup:** onions, shallots, carrots, celery, and garlic aromatic mix; tomatoes; broth; cream; rice vinegar. Top with some croutons.

**Carrot Soup:** leeks, onion, celery, garlic, and fresh ginger aromatic mix; carrots; broth; yogurt; lime juice.

**Broccoli or Asparagus Soup:** onions, leeks, and garlic aromatic mix; broccoli or asparagus; broth; cream; lemon juice. Top with crumbled crispy bacon.

**Butternut Squash Soup:** leeks, shallots, celery, and garlic aromatic mix; butternut squash; broth; yogurt; lime juice.

# Creamy Tomato Soup

**Natasha grew up on canned tomato soup, which she loved. It was a total treat, especially with buttered toast. But as an adult, she wanted a less processed version, and here it is. This is a very filling, rich soup. Add some cooked rice, if you like, or leave the cream out and serve the soup chilled in the summertime.**

One 28-ounce can diced tomatoes
2 teaspoons sugar
¼ teaspoon paprika
¼ teaspoon white pepper
½ teaspoon chopped fresh basil, or more to taste
3 sprigs flat-leaf parsley
1 teaspoon dried marjoram
1 bay leaf
3 tablespoon unsalted butter
1 cup chicken stock
2 tablespoons all-purpose flour
2 cups half-and-half
Kosher salt
2 tablespoons minced flat-leaf parsley for garnish

1 Combine the tomatoes, sugar, paprika, white pepper, herbs, 1 tablespoon of the butter, and the chicken stock in a saucepan. Simmer for about 10 minutes. Remove and discard the bay leaf; transfer the soup to a blender and purée.

2 In a pot, melt the remaining 2 tablespoons butter until bubbly. Add the flour, whisk together, and cook over low heat for a minute, to cook the flour. Gradually whisk in the half-and-half and cook, stirring, until smooth and thickened, about 5 minutes.

3 Add the puréed tomato mixture to the half-and-half mixture and simmer, stirring occasionally, for 10 minutes. Season with salt and add additional basil, if desired. Garnish with minced parsley.

**Serves 6**

# Scallion Soup

**This is a recipe from Alice's mother-in-law. In her family, this is called "Chi Chi Soup" because it is her eldest's favorite soup. Chi Chi has been asking her grandmother for "her" special soup ever since she was little, and of course, Grandma always is happy to add it to the weekend lunch table.**

2 tablespoons unsalted butter
1 tablespoon olive oil
5 large bunches trimmed scallions, thinly sliced
1 russet potato, peeled and thinly sliced
6 cups chicken stock
Kosher salt and freshly ground black pepper
⅓ to ½ cup heavy cream

1 Heat the butter and olive oil in a large pot over medium-low heat. Add the scallions and cook, stirring occasionally, until soft but not browned, about 20 minutes.

2 Add the potatoes and chicken broth and bring to a boil over medium-high heat. Reduce the heat and simmer until the potatoes are very soft and beginning to fall apart, about 40 minutes. Turn off the heat, season with salt and pepper to taste, and let cool slightly.

3 Using an immersion blender, a regular blender, or a food processor, purée the soup until smooth and mix in the heavy cream. Serve the soup hot or cold.

**Serves 4 to 6**

# Summer Corn Chowder

**This delicious light and creamy soup is really a dressed-up, healthier version of another of Natasha's favorite childhood comfort foods—creamed corn. The key to the soup's success is fresh, sweet corn.**

3 tablespoons unsalted butter
2 large leeks, coarsely chopped, white and light green parts only
1 small, sweet Vidalia onion, chopped
4 cups fresh sweet corn kernels
1 red bell pepper, finely diced
2½ cups chicken stock
½ cup heavy cream (you can substitute whole or skim milk, if you prefer)
Kosher salt and freshly ground black pepper

1. In a medium pot, melt 2 tablespoons of the butter, add the leeks and onion, and sauté over medium heat for 5 minutes. Set aside ¾ cup of corn and add 3¼ cups of corn to the pot. Sauté the vegetables for 3 to 5 minutes, until the leeks and onion are soft; do not brown. Remove from the pot and set aside.
2. In the same pot, melt the remaining 1 tablespoon butter, add the bell pepper, and sauté until tender, about 5 minutes; do not brown. Set the bell pepper aside.
3. Add the onion-corn mixture, stock, cream, and salt and black pepper to taste to the jar of a blender and blend until smooth. Check the consistency. If you prefer a thinner soup, add a little more chicken stock.
4. Return the soup to the pot, add the reserved corn kernels, bring to a simmer, and heat over medium-low heat. Divide the soup among four soup bowls and sprinkle with the reserved bell pepper. Serve immediately.

**Serves 4**

# Split Pea Soup

**This recipe comes from California, where split pea soup is famous. Pea Soup Andersen's of Buellton, California, has built its fortunes on this ubiquitous comfort food. Just remember to stir the soup frequently, running a wooden spoon along the bottom of the pot to make sure that it doesn't stick and burn.**

1 tablespoon olive oil
1 medium onion, diced
¼ pound slab bacon, diced
2 garlic cloves, chopped
½ cup peeled, chopped carrots
½ cup chopped celery
1 cup green or yellow dried split peas
1 ham bone or smoked ham hock
1 bay leaf
6 cups chicken stock
Kosher salt and freshly ground black pepper

1. In a large stockpot, heat the olive oil over medium-high heat. Add the onions and bacon and cook until the onions are tender and translucent. Add the garlic and cook for 1 minute. Add the carrots, celery, split peas, ham bone, bay leaf, and stock. Season with salt and pepper.
2. Bring to a boil, reduce the heat, and simmer over low heat, uncovered, for 1½ to 2 hours, until the peas have completely softened and the soup has turned into a chunky purée. Stir occasionally while cooking to make certain the soup doesn't stick to the bottom of the pot and burn. Taste and add additional salt and pepper, if needed. Serve immediately.

**Serves 4 to 6**

# Tortilla Soup





**This is a clean and easy version of the Mexican classic. If you like your soup more tomatoey, add a tablespoon or two of tomato paste. And don't rush cooking the chicken; a gentle simmer yields tender pieces.**

4 cups chicken stock
1 boneless, skinless chicken breast
3 garlic cloves, thinly sliced
1 cup corn kernels
1 jalapeño pepper, thinly sliced (optional)
Kosher salt and freshly ground black pepper
1 small avocado
1 cup cherry tomatoes, chopped
2 tablespoons diced red onion
1 lime
½ cup fresh cilantro leaves
2 ounces tortilla chips

1 In a large pot over high heat, bring the stock to a boil. Reduce the heat to low, add the chicken breast, and simmer gently until cooked, about 15 minutes. Remove the chicken breast from the pot, let cool, shred, and set aside.

2 Add the garlic, corn kernels, and jalapeño to the pot and heat. Stir in the shredded chicken. Season to taste with salt and pepper.

3 Dice the avocado and toss with the tomatoes, red onion, and juice of half the lime. Slice the other half of the lime into 4 wedges.

4 Divide the soup among four bowls. Garnish with the avocado mixture, cilantro, tortilla chips, and lime wedges.

Serves 4

# Tuscan Bean Soup

**At least once every two weeks it is time to cook beans in the slow cooker. Be sure to always have the ingredients for this recipe on hand in your pantry and refrigerator. Make more beans than you need and freeze the extra.**

1 pound dried beans (great northern, cannellini, or flageolet)
1 yellow onion, chopped
2 celery stalks, diced
1 large carrot, diced
3 garlic cloves, minced
¼ cup olive oil
1 tablespoon dried oregano
1 tablespoon dried parsley
1 bay leaf
4 cups water
4 cups chicken or vegetable stock
Kosher salt and freshly ground black pepper
4 slices bacon (optional)
Parmesan cheese rind (optional)
1 tablespoon balsamic vinegar

1. Rinse the beans and cover generously with cold water by at least 2 inches. Immediately discard any floating beans. Soak the beans overnight.
2. On the following day, drain the beans. Add the beans and the remaining ingredients, except for the balsamic vinegar, to a 6-quart slow cooker. Cover and cook on low for 8 to 10 hours until the beans are tender.
3. Remove one-third of the soup, purée it, and return it to the cooker. Add the balsamic vinegar. Taste and add additional salt and pepper, if needed.

Serves 6 to 8

TOO MANY
COOKS
SPOIL
THE
BROTH

# Grilled Cheese Sandwich

**It's just bread, cheese, and butter—right? Really, what could be simpler than a grilled cheese sandwich? Yet this beloved American lunch food seems to have as many variations as it has devotees. There is first the question of bread: traditionalists may opt for airy white; but wheat, rye, and sourdough are just a few other favorites. The second thing to consider is the type of cheese—the classic, of course, is American cheese—but as long as it melts, you can be sure that someone somewhere has tried it. And lastly, when it comes to "extras," well, then the list is truly endless: everything from tomatoes and bacon to pickles and apples; if you can fit it between two slices of bread, you can add it to a grilled cheese sandwich.**

**In Natasha's house, her father was the grilled cheese maker. He stuck to the basics: two pieces of thinly sliced supermarket white bread, two pieces of American cheese, and a generous application of salted butter. The pan was always cast-iron and the heat was always medium-low. But her dad had a secret weapon: a heavy solid antique iron, which he used to weigh down the sandwich after the first flip. The effect was exquisite—an extremely thin, almost delicate, perfectly browned, crispy-on-the-outside, gooey-on-the-inside grilled cheese sandwich. Cut immediately into little triangles for little hands and served alongside a smoothie, it was an unrivaled after-school snack.**

4 tablespoons (½ stick) salted butter, at room temperature
8 slices bread
8 slices cheese
Pickles for serving

1. Butter the bread and make 2 sandwiches with 2 pieces of cheese per sandwich; the buttered side should be on the outside of the sandwiches.
2. Heat a large nonstick frying pan over medium heat for a few minutes. Place the sandwiches in the pan, cover, and cook until the cheese starts to melt and the bread is crisp and golden brown, about 2 minutes.
3. Flip each sandwich over and press firmly with a spatula to flatten slightly and crisp the opposite side. Cook for about 1 minute until golden brown and turn each sandwich again. Press with the spatula again to recrisp the bread, about 30 seconds.
4. Cut the sandwiches and serve immediately.

**Serves 4**

# It's a Wrap

**Try these combinations on a plain or flavored tortilla. To wrap, fold the bottom of the tortilla about one-fourth of the way up, then fold the left side over the middle and the right side over the left. Then finish rolling, pick it up, and sink your teeth into it!**

### Turkey BLT Wrap

⅛ pound thinly sliced roasted turkey
2 slices bacon, cooked
2 to 3 slices tomato
¼ cup shredded lettuce
1 tablespoon creamy peppercorn or ranch dressing

### Reuben Wrap

2 slices corned beef
1 slice Swiss cheese
3 tablespoons sauerkraut
1 tablespoon Thousand Island dressing

### Veggie Supreme Wrap

1 tablespoon herbed cream cheese
¼ avocado, sliced
¼ yellow bell pepper, cut into strips
2 to 3 slices tomato
4 to 6 spinach leaves
2 tablespoons grated carrot
2 tablespoons alfalfa sprouts

### Great Salad Wrap

2 leaves romaine lettuce
¼ recipe Great Tuna Salad (page 160) or Great Chicken Salad (page 161)

Makes 1 sandwich each

# Stuffed Pita Pockets





**Halved pita pockets are fun little vessels for all sorts of goodies. A ground meat mixture is an obvious choice. You can also use any left over taco fillings, left over turkey-veggie mixture (see page 236), or stuff with Quick Bean Salad with Lemony Tahini Sauce (see Variation, page 158).**

1 tablespoon olive oil
1 pound ground beef or ground turkey
1 tomato, diced
1 green bell pepper, diced
1 onion, diced
¾ cup bean sprouts
Kosher salt and freshly ground black pepper
4 pita rounds, halved
Shredded cheddar cheese

1. Heat the olive oil in a large cast-iron skillet over medium heat. Add the meat and cook, stirring, until it is no longer pink, about 5 minutes. Drain off excess fat.
2. Add the tomato, bell pepper, onion, bean sprouts, and salt and black pepper to taste. Sauté 5 to 10 minutes, until the meat is cooked and the vegetables are tender.
3. Stuff the mixture into the pita pockets and sprinkle with the cheese.

**Makes 8 small pita sandwiches**

# Sloppy Joes

**Oh, this is so messy and so good. As kids, Natasha and her sister ate Sloppy Joes over and over again. Their dad poured it over macaroni. He poured it over rice. He put in on English muffins and he served it on top of toast. They even used it as a sauce for lasagna. For the classic Sloppy Joe, serve on an open hamburger bun.**

2 tablespoons olive oil
2 onions, chopped
4 celery stalks, chopped
4 garlic cloves, chopped
2 pounds lean ground beef
1 cup tomato sauce, canned or homemade
3 tablespoons tomato paste
½ cup ketchup
1 teaspoon Tabasco sauce
2 teaspoons Worcestershire sauce
Kosher salt and freshly ground black pepper
4 whole wheat hamburger buns

1. Heat the oil in a large, heavy, cast-iron skillet over low heat. Add the onions and celery and cook until soft and lightly browned. Add the garlic and continue cooking for 3 to 4 minutes.
2. Increase the heat to medium-high and add the ground beef. Cook, stirring occasionally to break up any large pieces, for 10 to 12 minutes, until the meat is browned.
3. Reduce the heat to medium and add the tomato sauce, tomato paste, ketchup, and Tabasco and Worcestershire sauces. Cook, stirring, for 15 to 30 minutes until the liquid has reduced and the mixture has thickened. Season with salt and pepper to taste. Serve on hamburger buns, preferably with a knife and fork—it will be messy!

**Serves 4**

# What's in That Lunch Bag?

**When Alice's eldest daughter Chi Chi was in second grade, she had a pickle for lunch practically every day for a stretch because she didn't like anything else the cafeteria was serving. It drove Alice batty. There are definitely times when you need to send your kids out the door with packed lunches.**

## LUNCH BAG STUFFERS

Invest in some good thermoses in various sizes to keep soups or leftover dinners warm for several hours, or smoothies and salads nice and cool. The following is a list of recipes from the book that can be successfully packed for lunches.

- A Whirl of Smoothies
- Homemade Applesauce
- Kitchen Sink Frittata
- Whole Wheat Banana Nut Waffles
- Great Granola
- Banana Oatmeal Muffins
- Rice and Beans
- Macaroni and Cheese
- Risotto with Zucchini and Peas
- Chicken Fingers
- Broiled Salmon
- Pan-fried Salmon Rice Cakes
- Turkey Chili
- Basic Roasted Vegetables
- Five-Star Salad Bar
- Fried Farro with Collard Greens
- Quinoa with Fennel and Pine Nuts
- Cookies
- Brownies
- Lemon Squares
- Marshmallow Rice Treats
- P B & J Bars
- Quick Breads

- Most of the recipes from the Soup & Sandwiches and Snacks & Small Bites sections!

## LUNCH BAG ADDITIONS

- Milk
- Diluted juice
- Water
- Apples
- Bananas
- Berries
- Cubed melon
- Peeled oranges
- Baby carrots
- Celery sticks
- Yogurt cups
- Pudding cups
- Crackers with sliced cheese and salami
- String cheese
- Popcorn
- Pretzels
- Hard-boiled eggs
- Edamame
- Sunflower seeds
- Granola bars
- Fig bars
- Dried fruits

## FIVE FABULOUS LUNCHES

It doesn't have to be sandwiches everyday. Think leftover dinners; items like frittatas, soups, muffins, and treats you can make over the weekend and freeze; a few easy items you can prepare in the morning; add veggie sticks, fresh fruit, and dips . . . mix and match and the possibilities are endless. Here are a few combinations for inspiration:

- Favorite soup in a thermos, Banana Oatmeal Muffin (page 90), fresh fruit, and milk.
- Orange-Yogurt Smoothie (page 58) in a thermos, favorite wrap (page 121), Pumpkin Bar (page 335), and water.
- Cold Sesame Noodles (page 166), Favorite Yogurt Dip (page 144), veggie sticks and fresh fruit slices, and milk.
- Leftover dinner in a thermos, salad with Caesar dressing (page 275) on the side, Marshmallow Rice Treats (page 328), and diluted juice.
- Mini Frittata (page 173), leftover Roasted Vegetables (page 256), favorite Dip/Dressing (page 201), and diluted juice.

## LUNCH BAG SAFETY & TIPS



- Perishable foods must be kept cold. These include cooked meats such as cold cuts, as well as premade tuna salads, chicken salads, and egg salads. All of these foods are potential targets for the bacteria that cause food poisoning.
- Soft, insulated lunch bags or boxes with an ice pack or frozen gel packs are the best choices for keeping lunches cold.
- Thermoses can be used for more than just juice—keep hot foods warm for several hours, or smoothies and salads cold.
- Keep lettuce, tomatoes, and other "moist" foods wrapped separately. Build your sandwich at lunchtime and avoid soggy sammies!
- Pack salad dressing in a separate container so leafy greens don't turn soggy.
- Pack travel-size moist hand wipes for easy cleanup.
- Leftovers that are brought home might not be safe to eat because of length of time above temperature of 40°F. "When in doubt, throw it out."
- It is safest not to reuse sandwich bags, aluminum foil, and plastic wrap that's been sitting in lunch bags all day. They can contaminate other food and cause food borne illness.
- Insulated lunch bags, lunch boxes, and reuseable food containers should be washed with hot soapy water after each use.

# Portobello, Mozzarella, and Pesto Press





**Portobello mushrooms will shrink after cooking and become the perfect size to fit on a hamburger bun. Thick and meaty, portobellos in a sandwich are a good way to introduce mushrooms to finicky eaters. Add mozzarella and pesto, use a panini press, and presto—a warm vegetarian sandwich for your family.**

4 medium portobello mushrooms
2 tablespoons plus 2 teaspoons olive oil
Kosher salt and freshly ground black pepper
½ cup Pesto Sauce (see page 252)
4 whole wheat hamburger rolls
4 ounces mozzarella cheese

1 Preheat the oven to 400°F.

2 Remove the stems and wipe the mushroom caps clean with damp paper towels. Using a spoon, scrape off the gills from the underside of the mushrooms. Place the mushrooms, cap side down, on a baking sheet and drizzle with the olive oil. Season with salt and pepper to taste. Roast the mushrooms in the oven until tender, about 15 minutes.

3 Spread 2 tablespoons of pesto on the bottom of each roll and top each with a roasted mushroom and 1 ounce of the cheese. Top each sandwich with the other half of the roll and brush both sides of the roll with the remaining 2 teaspoons oil.

4 Heat a panini or sandwich press according to the manufacturer's instructions, or a large cast-iron skillet over medium-high heat. Cook the sandwiches two at a time in the press or skillet until golden brown and crisp, 5 to 8 minutes. If using the skillet, press the sandwiches down with a heavy pan and flip them halfway through the cooking time. Serve immediately.

**Serves 4**

**Variations** For more sophisticated tastes, try making the sandwich with portobello mushrooms, goat cheese, and roasted red peppers. For simpler tastes, try portobello mushrooms, cheddar cheese, and tomato slices.

# Chicken and Bean Quesadillas

**This recipe stretches any leftover meat from the previous night's dinner. Add a can of beans, flavorings, and of course a bit of cheese. Crisp up the sandwich, and no one will say "Mommm . . . we just had that for dinner!"**

2 cups leftover cooked chicken, pork, or beef, shredded
One 15-ounce can black beans, rinsed and drained
½ cup coarsely chopped fresh cilantro
Four 7-inch flour tortillas
1 cup grated melting cheese, such as cheddar or Monterey Jack
2 tablespoons canola oil
Guacamole (page 146)

1. Preheat the oven to 200°F.
2. In a large bowl, toss together the meat, beans, and cilantro. Top half of each tortilla with one-fourth of the mixture and the cheese. Fold the uncovered half of the tortilla over the filling.
3. Heat 1 tablespoon of the oil in a medium cast-iron skillet over medium heat. Add 2 quesadillas to the skillet and weigh down with a small pot lid. Cook for 2 to 3 minutes, until golden brown, then flip and crisp the opposite side, about 2 minutes more. Transfer the quesadillas to the oven to keep them warm and repeat the procedure to make the remaining quesadillas.
4. Cut the quesadillas into wedges and serve with guacamole on the side.

**Serves 4**

# Cuban Sandwich

**Cubano, or a Cuban sandwich, is Alice and her daughter Sylvia's favorite sandwich. It is essentially a Latin variation on a grilled ham-and-cheese sandwich, but with more salty, savory goodness from extra spices and pickles.**

1 garlic clove, minced and mashed
1 tablespoon olive oil
1 tablespoon freshly squeezed lime juice
1 tablespoon chopped fresh cilantro
4 oval-shaped small hero rolls
2 tablespoons grainy mustard
8 ounces sliced ham
8 ounces roasted pork, sliced, or substitute turkey slices
4 slices Swiss cheese
2 large dill pickles, sliced
2 tablespoons unsalted butter, softened

1 In a small bowl, combine the garlic, oil, lime juice, and cilantro. Let sit for 5 minutes.

2 Split the rolls in half horizontally. Spread a bit of the garlic mixture and mustard on the bottom halves, divide the ham, pork, cheese, and pickle slices among the 4 sandwiches, and top with the upper halves of the rolls.

3 Butter the tops and bottoms of the sandwiches.

4 Preheat a panini or sandwich press according to the manufacturer's instructions, or a large cast-iron skillet over medium-high heat. Cook the sandwiches in the press or skillet, two at a time, until golden brown and crisp, 8 to 10 minutes. If using the skillet, press the sandwiches down with a heavy pan, and flip halfway through the cooking time. Serve immediately.

**Serves 4**

# Shrimp Salad Rolls

**Frozen shrimp, like frozen vegetables (see page 304), are often "fresher" than the frozen and thawed shrimp sitting at the supermarket. For special occasions, toss together this yummy treat.**

1 pound large shrimp
¾ cup chopped celery
½ cup mayonnaise
1 tablespoon chopped fresh tarragon
Kosher salt and freshly ground black pepper
2 tablespoons unsalted butter, softened
4 whole wheat hot dog buns

1 Bring a large pot of salted water to a boil, add the shrimp, and cook until bright pink, about 2 minutes. Drain and cool the shrimp under cold running water. Peel, devein, and cut into ½-inch pieces.

2 In a large bowl, mix the celery, mayonnaise, tarragon, and salt and pepper to taste. Stir in the shrimp and chill, covered, in the refrigerator for 30 minutes.

3 Heat a large cast-iron skillet over medium-low heat. Lightly butter both sides of the buns. Place them in the pan and toast for about 2 minutes on each side until golden brown.

4 Stuff the buns with the shrimp salad and serve immediately.

Serves 4

# Fish Sandwich Rolls

**Fish with tartar sauce is a classic combination. Pan-fry breaded fish until crispy and serve in soft hot dog buns for a textural contrast.**

1 pound Pan-fried Fish (page 218)
4 whole wheat hot dog buns
Lettuce leaves (optional)
Sliced tomatoes (optional)

**Tartar Sauce**
½ cup mayonnaise
1 tablespoon sweet pickle relish
½ dill pickle, finely chopped
1 tablespoon finely chopped onion
1 tablespoon chopped fresh dill
1 to 2 tablespoons freshly squeezed lemon juice

1. In a small bowl, combine all of the ingredients for the tartar sauce and mix well. Cover and refrigerate.
2. Prepare Steps 1 and 2 of Pan-Fried Fish, or use leftovers. Cut the fish into 1½-inch-wide strips.
3. Slather the bottom halves of the hot dog buns with the tartar sauce. Add the fish strips and the lettuce and tomato, if using. Cover with the upper halves of the buns.

**Serves 4**

# Snacks & Small Bites

# Easy Nibblies

**Keep canned chickpeas in the cupboard, spiced nuts in a jar, and edamame in the freezer for snack attacks. High in protein, fiber, and other nutrients, any of these easy nibblies are excellent to have anytime.**

## Roasted Chickpeas

One 15-ounce can chickpeas
1½ tablespoons olive oil
Kosher salt
Creole seasoning, chili powder, or favorite spice blend

1. Preheat the oven to 400°F.
2. Drain and rinse the chickpeas. Pat the chickpeas dry with paper towels and toss with the oil and a bit of kosher salt. Roast the chickpeas on a baking sheet until golden brown and crunchy, 30 to 45 minutes, stirring occasionally.
3. Sprinkle with creole seasoning, chili powder, or your favorite spice blend, if desired. Let cool slightly before serving. The chickpeas may be kept in an airtight container for 3 days at room temperature.

**Makes 1 cup**

## Spiced Nuts

2 cups favorite nut mix
1 tablespoon unsalted butter
2 tablespoons brown sugar
¼ teaspoon each ground cumin, cayenne, ground cinnamon, kosher salt

1 Heat the nuts in a dry skillet and stir and toast over medium heat for about 5 minutes. Remove from the skillet and set aside.

2 Add the butter, 1 tablespoon water, sugar, and spices to the hot pan and heat for about a minute. Return the nuts to the pan and cook, stirring, for 1 or 2 minutes, until a glaze forms. Cool and store in an airtight container.

**Makes 2 cups**

## Easy Edamame (Soy Beans)

One 12-ounce package frozen edamame in pods, or fresh
Sea salt

Boil fresh or frozen edamame in their pods just until tender, 4 to 6 minutes. Drain and sprinkle with sea salt. To eat, squeeze out the beans from the pods for little snackers. Older kids and adults can eat them the traditional way, using their teeth to pinch the beans out from the pods.

**Makes 2 cups**

**Good to Know** Edamame (soybeans) provide more protein than other beans and contain all the essential amino acids your body needs. It is as complete a protein as meat, but without the saturated fat and cholesterol. Toss cooked and shelled edamame into salads, or try roasting them.

# Nuts and Seeds

**Plentiful in protein, nuts and seeds are great snack options and excellent additions to many dishes, providing benefits like the antioxidant vitamin E and fiber. The flavonoids found in the skins of nuts boost the body's immune system, by fueling beneficial bacteria in the GI tract, and help prevent cell damage. But this subgroup's greatest claim to fame is its potential ability to lower your risk for heart disease.**

## DID YOU KNOW?

Nuts are really hard-rinded fruits or the kernels found inside a fruit, and seeds are broadly defined as small, dry fruits.

## FAT BLOCKERS

Believe it or not, it's the healthy monounsaturated fat components in nuts—called phytosterols—that are responsible for lowering "bad" LDL cholesterol through blocking the body's absorption of it.

## MEAT SUBSTITUTE

Pound for pound, nuts are right up there with meat sources for protein and fat content. Three tablespoons of peanut butter is equivalent to a good-size portion of meat; so that P B & J sandwich you ate for lunch may give you as much as one meat serving. Remember, though, that the fat in nuts is different. Unlike that of meat, it's largely monounsaturated and will not raise bad cholesterol.

## NUTTY OILS

Today's supermarket presents an array of cooking oils including walnut oil, peanut oil, sesame oil, and even pistachio oil. Among these, walnut oil is the only one that provides

substantial amounts of alpha-linolenic acid, or ALA, an omega-3 fatty acid. The body can't produce its own ALA, but uses ALA from walnuts to improve LDL-to-HDL ratios. This oil has a shorter shelf life before going rancid, however, so store it in the fridge and use it frequently. Walnut oil is better used for adding flavor than for cooking longer term, as high temperatures tend to give it a bitter taste.

## STORING

Keep in mind that the higher the fat content in nuts and seeds, the more quickly they will go rancid. Nuts stored in the fridge in airtight containers can last up to 6 months, while nuts kept in the freezer won't spoil for up to a year. Pecans are the most delicate of all, and won't last long once shelled.

| | | |
|---|---|---|
| WALNUTS | • highest in ALA, gamma-tocopherol, and cancer-fighting ellagic acid<br>• nongreasy oil is prized for use in massage and skin treatment as well as on salad, pasta, or fish | Tip: Buy whole or halved: the greater surface area exposed by little pieces encourages spoilage. |
| ALMONDS | • high in vitamin E, a natural blood thinner; the flavonoids quercitin and anthocyanin, and magnesium and calcium<br>• delicate oil provides oleic acid and is also used cosmetically | Fact: Almond oil, though expensive, is higher in healthy fat than peanut oil, and is suitable for frying. |
| PECANS | • rich in the amino acid L-arginine, which may promote arterial health<br>• oil has a high smoking point, making it suitable for grilling meat or poultry | Fact: An American nut, the pecan comes from the hickory tree. |
| PISTACHIOS | • packed with potassium, oleic acid, and antioxidants<br>• split or roasted, crushed nuts are a great addition to salads, desserts, and ice cream | Tip: Buy unsalted, undyed (greenish) nuts in shells for the highest quality. |
| FLAXSEED | • high in ALA, fiber, and lignans, phytoestrogens that may fight hormone-positive breast cancers when eaten freshly ground | Tip: For health benefits, grind whole seeds in a spice grinder just before consuming. |

| | | |
|---|---|---|
| | • Flaxseed, or linseed, oil has a strong odor and flavor, which makes it unpopular for consumption except as a supplement | |
| **PUMPKIN SEEDS** | • endowed with lots of zinc and magnesium, as well as phytosterols to lower cholesterol<br>• delicious toasted in a skillet over medium heat for a minute or two<br>• oil is best as flavoring; cooking destroys its essential fatty acids | Tip: Eat in the white outer shell for the phytosterols. |
| **SESAME SEEDS** | • range from creamy white to black<br>• exceptionally abundant in iron, magnesium, and calcium, and contain a lignan called sesamin | Tip: Nutrients are better absorbed when seeds are ground or pulverized before consumption, as in tahini. |
| **GRAPE SEEDS** | • perhaps the most studied of all seeds for their antioxidant impact, are currently being looked at for their cancer-fighting resveratrol content, blood-pressure-lowering ability, wound-healing effects, as a remedy for edema, and more<br>• oil is ideal for all kinds of frying and cooking | Fact: Resveratrol is almost absent in the cold-pressed oil, but is present in grape-seed extract. |

# Popcorn Munchies

**Sometimes only munchies with a bit of salt will do, but that doesn't mean they can't come with fiber (in the popcorn and wheat squares), protein (in the nuts), and antioxidants (in the dried cranberries and dark chocolate chips).**

4 tablespoons (½ stick) unsalted butter
4 cups popped popcorn
2 cups shredded wheat cereal squares
1 cup walnut pieces or slivered almonds
Kosher salt
½ cup dried cranberries
½ cup dark-chocolate chips

1 Preheat the oven to 250°F. In 13 x 9-inch pan, melt the butter in the preheating oven.

2 In large bowl, combine the popcorn, wheat squares, and walnuts. Pour the butter over the dry ingredients and toss. Season to taste with the kosher salt.

3 Bake for 1 hour, stirring every 15 minutes. Cool completely and add the cranberries and chocolate. Store in an airtight container.

**Makes 8 cups**

# Popcorn Toppers

**Toss 4 cups of popped popcorn with any of the following fun flavor combinations.**

### Zesty Popcorn

¼ cup grated Parmesan cheese
1 tablespoon Italian seasoning
4 teaspoons melted unsalted butter
1 cup crumbled Baked Kale Chips (page 148)

### Cheesy Popcorn

¼ cup grated sharp cheese
4 teaspoons melted unsalted butter
½ teaspoon garlic salt

### Cinnamon Popcorn

1 tablespoon sugar
1½ teaspoons ground cinnamon
2 tablespoons melted unsalted butter

### Tex-Mex Popcorn

1 teaspoon chili powder
1 teaspoon paprika
1 teaspoon ground cumin
2 tablespoons melted unsalted butter

### Mexican Popcorn

2 tablespoons melted unsalted butter
1 tablespoon taco seasoning

### Sweet and Nutty

2 tablespoons melted unsalted butter
1 tablespoon brown sugar
½ cup roasted peanuts or almonds

# Veggie and Fruit Yogurt Dips

**A little dipping action can make veggies and fruits disappear. Try these or the Tahini-Yogurt Dressing used in Baba Ganoush (page 147). For a hummus dip and some extra protein, add 2 cups mashed, canned chickpeas to the tahini dressing.**

**Ranch-Yogurt Veggie Dip**

¾ cup plain yogurt
⅓ cup mayonnaise
1 tablespoon minced, flat-leaf parsley
2 tablespoons ranch seasoning

**Mustard-Yogurt Veggie Dip**

¾ cup plain yogurt
¼ cup Dijon mustard
Juice of 1 lemon

**Honey-Yogurt Fruit Dip**

1 cup plain yogurt
3 tablespoons honey
½ teaspoon vanilla extract
½ teaspoon almond extract

1 Mix the ingredients for each dip thoroughly and set in the refrigerator to chill.

2 Serve the veggie dips with cut raw or lightly steamed vegetables, such as plum tomatoes, bell peppers, broccoli, cauliflower, green beans, sugar snaps, celery, and carrots; and the fruit dip with grapes, berries, sliced bananas, mandarin orange segments, sliced kiwi, or melon cubes.

**Makes about 1 cup each**

# Guacamole

**This south-of-the-border favorite goes well with virtually any Mexican-style dish and is great as a dip for chips or veggies. What's more, it's really good for you! Avocados are an excellent cholesterol-free, sodium-free food that supplies more nutrients for fewer calories than any other fruit.**

2 to 3 ripe avocados, pitted and peeled
1 tomato, chopped
1 jalapeño pepper, seeds and membranes removed and discarded, finely chopped (optional)
¼ cup chopped red onions or scallions
¼ cup minced fresh cilantro
2 teaspoons freshly squeezed lemon or lime juice
Kosher salt

In a large bowl, mash the avocados and stir in the remaining ingredients until blended.

**Makes about 3 cups**

**Tip** To stop homemade guacamole from turning brown before you serve it, reserve the avocado pit and place it in the mixture, then squeeze fresh lemon juice over the surface. Cover the guacamole with plastic wrap pressed directly on the surface to prevent oxidation.

# Baba Ganoush





**Eggplant is a very good source of fiber and is high in folic acid and potassium. Technically a fruit, eggplant has a fairly neutral flavor; it is the pulpy texture kids need to get used to. Entice picky eaters to try eggplant at snack time by serving this Middle Eastern dip with Homemade Pita Chips (page 150) or crackers. The tahini is usually stronger in traditional recipes, but here the yogurt lightens the flavor a little.**

1 large eggplant, about 1 pound
2 to 4 tablespoons tahini
2 tablespoons freshly squeezed lemon juice
½ cup plain nonfat yogurt
½ to 1 garlic clove, minced and mashed
2 teaspoons ground cumin
1 teaspoon paprika
Kosher salt

1 Preheat the oven to 400°F. Prick the eggplant about a dozen times with a fork and place on a lightly oiled baking sheet. (Do not skip this skip or the eggplant will burst in the oven.) Bake until soft inside, about 30 to 40 minutes, turning twice. Let cool.

2 Cut the eggplant in half lengthwise, drain any liquid, and scoop out the pulp. Chop the pulp well, or process in a food processer, and transfer to a bowl.

3 In a separate bowl, mix 2 tablespoons tahini, lemon juice, and yogurt until smooth. Stir in the garlic, cumin, paprika, and salt.

4 Add the tahini-yogurt dressing to the eggplant and combine thoroughly. Taste and add more tahini if desired. Refrigerate for 3 hours to allow flavors to blend. Serve cold or at room temperature.

**Makes about 1½ cups**

# Baked Kale Chips

**Try these—they are just as addictive as potato chips. Introduce them to little ones early and add nutritious kale to their diet regularly.** **See Great Greens Sauté (page 284) for nutritional information.**

1 bunch kale
2 tablespoons olive oil
Sea salt
¼ teaspoon pimentón (smoked paprika) (optional)
¼ teaspoon granulated garlic (optional)
1 tablespoon grated Parmesan cheese (optional)

1. Preheat the oven to 275°F.
2. Remove the stems and tough center ribs from the kale and tear the leaves into bite-size pieces. Rinse and thoroughly dry the leaves—the leaves should be really dry! Toss with the olive oil and salt and arrange in a single layer on baking sheets.
3. Bake until the leaves are crisp but still dark green—they get bitter when they turn brown—turning the leaves halfway through the baking time, about 20 to 30 minutes total.
4. Sprinkle with the paprika and granulated garlic or with grated Parmesan cheese, if desired. Serve as finger food or crumble over popcorn.

**Serves 2 to 4**

# Sweet Potato Chips

**Instead of opening a bag of chips, make these Sweet Potato Chips for the extra vitamin A and fiber. Also see Sweet Potato Fries (page 302).**

3 medium sweet potatoes, about 1 pound, scrubbed
2 tablespoons crumbled dried herbs or spices, such as dill, rosemary, onion flakes, or chili powder
½ teaspoon garlic salt
¼ teaspoon freshly ground black pepper
Nonstick cooking spray
1 tablespoon olive oil

1 Preheat the oven to 425°F.

2 Cut the sweet potatoes into very thin slices and pat dry with paper towels.

3 In a small bowl, combine the herbs, garlic salt, and pepper. Set aside.

4 Coat a baking sheet with nonstick cooking spray and arrange the potato slices in a single layer on the sheet.

5 Spray the potato slices with more cooking spray. Bake for 15 minutes.

6 Turn the slices over and brush with the olive oil. Sprinkle the herb (or spice) mixture evenly onto the slices. Bake for 15 to 20 minutes more, until the chips are crisp and golden. Cool on the baking sheet before serving.

**Serves 4 to 6**

# Homemade Pita Chips

**Serve these pita chips with Baba Ganoush (page 147) or a hummus dip (page 144). Pack lunchboxes with pita chips, red bell pepper strips, sliced cucumbers, or baby carrots and a dip, all in separate containers to prevent sogginess.**

- 8 pocket pita breads, preferably whole wheat
- ¼ cup olive oil
- Sea salt and freshly ground black pepper
- Grated Parmesan cheese (optional)

1. Preheat the oven to 400°F.
2. Cut the pita bread into 8 triangles. For crispier chips, slit each pita bread in half before cutting into triangles—these are great to munch on but less sturdy for dipping.
3. Place the triangles on a baking sheet and brush both sides lightly with a bit of olive oil. Bake for about 10 to 15 minutes until crispy (split pita bread will take less time).
4. Sprinkle with sea salt, pepper, and Parmesan cheese, if desired.

**Serves 4 to 6**

## Variation

**Substitute:** ½ teaspoon garlic salt, ¼ teaspoon dried basil, and ½ teaspoon dried chervil for the Parmesan cheese.

# Homemade Tortilla Chips

**Serve these tortilla chips with Seven-Layer Dip (page 156), Guaca-Salsa (Tip, page 307), or Avocado, Corn, and Black Bean Salsa (page 262).**

- 1 dozen 6-inch corn tortillas, quartered
- 2 tablespoons olive oil
- Sea salt

1. Preheat the oven to 400°F.
2. Cut each tortilla into 6 triangles. Place the triangles on a baking sheet and brush both sides lightly with a bit of olive oil. Bake for 8 to 10 minutes until crispy.
3. Sprinkle with sea salt to taste.

**Serves 4 to 6**

# Cheesy Potato Skins

**Potato skins have a lot of fiber and nutrients. Make Cheesy Potato Skins when you need just the pulp for puréed soups.**

2 medium baking potatoes
2 tablespoons unsalted butter, at room temperature
1 cup grated cheddar cheese
4 slices turkey bacon, cooked and crumbled
¼ cup sour cream
2 tablespoons chopped, pitted black olives
2 tablespoons minced fresh chives (optional)

1 Preheat the oven to 425°F.

2 Scrub the potatoes well and pierce with a fork. Bake on the bottom rack of the oven for 1 hour, or until tender when tested with a fork. Set the potatoes aside until cool enough to handle.

3 Cut the potatoes in half lengthwise. Using a large spoon, scoop out the center of each potato, leaving a ½-inch-thick shell. Reserve the scooped-out potato pulp for soup or Heavenly Hash Browns (page 84).

4 Quarter the potato halves. Then cut the quarters in half to create 16 triangular wedges. Arrange the potato skins on a baking sheet.

5 Brush the insides of the potato skins with butter and bake for 8 to 12 minutes until golden and crispy.

6 Remove from the oven and sprinkle the potato skins with the cheese. Bake for another 5 minutes, or until the cheese has melted.

7 Sprinkle the crumbled bacon on top of each potato skin, add a dollop of sour cream, and top with the chopped olives and minced chives. Serve hot.

**Serves 6 to 8**

**Variation** Follow the recipe for the potato skins through Step 5. Serve with Seven-Layer Dip (page 156) or Veggie Dips (page 144).

# Potato Crisps

**This is a satisfying vessel for Seven-Layer Dip (page 156) or Veggie Dips (page 144).**

2 large baking potatoes, scrubbed and cut into thin slices
2 tablespoons vegetable oil
Kosher salt
Grated cheese or mixed dried herbs (optional)

1 Preheat the oven to 375°F.
2 Arrange the potato slices on a rimmed baking sheet and brush both sides with vegetable oil. Sprinkle with salt.
3 Bake for 30 minutes, or until golden brown and crispy.
4 Remove from the oven. Using a spatula, flip the potatoes over and sprinkle with more salt.
5 Return to the oven and bake for another 15 to 20 minutes until golden brown.
6 Sprinkle with grated cheese or mixed dried herbs, if using, and let cool to room temperature before serving.

**Serves 4 to 6**

POTATO
QUICKSTEP

# Seven-Layer Dip





**The term "refried beans" is actually a mistranslation of *frijoles refritos,* the name of a popular Mexican dish. The beans are usually cooked and mashed, then baked or fried once—and like all beans, they are a good source of fiber and protein. Canned versions are a good addition to your pantry—just check the sodium content—some brands are healthier than others.**

One 16-ounce can low-sodium refried beans
One 12-ounce jar salsa
8 ounces sour cream
2 cups shredded iceberg lettuce
2 cups diced tomatoes
2 cups shredded cheddar cheese
One 6-ounce can pitted black olives

In a microwave-safe serving dish, layer the beans, salsa, sour cream, lettuce, tomatoes, cheese, and olives. Microwave on high power for 2 to 3 minutes until the cheese is just melted. Serve immediately with Potato Crisps (page 154) or Homemade Tortilla Chips (page 151).

**Serves 6**

# Super Nachos

One 16-ounce can low-sodium refried beans
1 tablespoon taco seasoning
2 cups diced tomatoes
2 tablespoons fresh minced cilantro
2 ripe avocados
2 teaspoons lemon juice
One 13-ounce bag tortilla chips, or Homemade Tortilla Chips (page 151)
½ cup grated Monterey Jack cheese
½ cup grated cheddar cheese
½ cup sour cream
3 jalapeño peppers, seeded, membranes removed, minced (optional)

1. Preheat the oven to 400°F.
2. In a saucepan, mix together the refried beans and taco seasoning. Cook over medium heat until bubbly. Remove from the heat.
3. In a small bowl, combine the tomatoes and cilantro.
4. In a separate bowl, mash the avocados with the lemon juice until well blended.
5. Spread the chips out evenly on a large baking sheet or ovenproof platter. Spread a layer of the refried beans on top of the chips. Sprinkle the grated cheeses over the beans. Spread the tomatoes and cilantro evenly over the top. Bake for 3 to 5 minutes, until the cheese has melted.
6. Spoon the avocado mixture on top of the nachos and top with the sour cream. Sprinkle with the minced jalapeños, if using. Eat immediately!

**Serves 8 to 10**

# Quick Bean Salad

**This is the first dish Alice's kids learned how to make on their own. They love it for an after-school snack and any time they are hungry and their mother is busy!**

3 tablespoons rice vinegar or 2 tablespoons balsamic vinegar
2 tablespoons Dijon mustard
6 tablespoons extra-virgin olive oil
One 15-ounce can beans of your choice, rinsed and drained, or 1½ cups of your favorite cooked bean mix
½ cup small-dice red bell pepper
½ cup small-dice cucumber
½ cup minced flat-leaf parsley

1 In a small bowl, combine the vinegar and mustard, then slowly whisk in the olive oil until well emulsified.

2 In a medium bowl, toss the remaining ingredients together and mix in the vinaigrette. Serve the salad at room temperature or chilled.

**Serves 6**

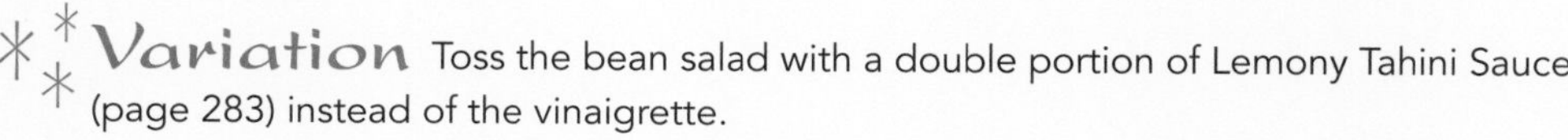

**Variation** Toss the bean salad with a double portion of Lemony Tahini Sauce (page 283) instead of the vinaigrette.

# Great Tuna Salad

**Tuna fish is a nutrient-dense food, a source of high-quality protein, and rich in omega-3 essential fatty acids. Canned tuna is a convenient item to have in your pantry, but you should be aware of mercury level warnings. Choose canned light tuna, which has less mercury than canned white or albacore tuna. Parents should limit their young children's intake of canned light tuna to three meals per month.**

Two 6-ounce cans light tuna, packed in water
2 tablespoons freshly squeezed lemon juice
1 small celery stalk, minced
2 tablespoons minced red onion
2 tablespoons minced sweet pickle
½ cup mayonnaise, or a mixture of yogurt and mayonnaise
½ teaspoon Dijon mustard
Kosher salt and freshly ground black pepper

1 Drain the tuna and shred well with a fork until no clumps remain and the texture is smooth; this prevents bites of dry, unseasoned tuna.

2 In a bowl, mix the tuna with the remaining ingredients until well combined. Serve over a bed of mixed greens, or make sandwiches. The tuna salad can be covered and refrigerated for up to 3 days.

**Serves 4**

## Variations

**Tuna Salad with Grapes and Almonds:** Omit the lemon juice and pickles and add 2 tablespoons balsamic vinegar, 1 cup halved seedless grapes, and ¼ cup toasted slivered almonds.

**Curried Tuna Salad:** Omit the pickles and mix 1 tablespoon curry powder into the mayonnaise. Add 1 cup diced apple and ¼ cup raisins.

**Great Chicken Salad:** Substitute shredded meat from 2 cooked chicken breasts for the tuna in any of the recipes.

# Eggs, Pesto, and Pasta Salad

**The pasta salads on these pages can be easily adapted to suit your personal taste and to use whatever ingredients you have available. Add left-over chicken, roasted vegetables, and/or bean salad. They are great to have in the refrigerator for a quick snack or to pack into lunchboxes.**

½ pound green beans, trimmed and halved crosswise
6 hard-boiled eggs, peeled and quartered
½ pound whole wheat spiral pasta, cooked until al dente
½ cup Pesto Sauce (page 252) or store-bought

1 In a large saucepan of boiling water, blanch the green beans for 3 to 5 minutes, just until tender, then drain.

2 In a bowl, toss together all of the ingredients for the salad and combine well. Serve warm or at room temperature.

**Serves 4**

# Whole Wheat Pasta Salad

1 pound whole wheat tubular pasta
¼ cup olive oil
2 tablespoons balsamic vinegar
1 garlic clove, minced
1 cup frozen corn kernels
1 cup frozen peas
½ cup finely chopped sun-dried tomatoes
¼ cup chopped scallions
Kosher salt and freshly ground black pepper
½ cup grated Parmesan cheese

1 Bring a large pot of salted water to a rapid boil and cook the pasta according to the package instructions until al dente. Drain and set aside.

2 Whisk together the olive oil, balsamic vinegar, and garlic.

3 In a medium saucepan, bring 3 cups of water to a boil and add the frozen corn and peas. Boil the vegetables for 2 minutes, just until tender and drain.

4 In a large bowl, combine the pasta, corn kernels, peas, sun-dried tomatoes, and scallions, and toss with the dressing. Season with salt and pepper to taste. Let cool, then sprinkle with the grated cheese. Serve the salad at room temperature or chilled.

**Serves 4 to 6**

# Whole-Grain Salad
## with Roasted Vegetables

**Make a practice of preparing extra Quinoa with Fennel (page 310) and Basic Roasted Vegetables (page 256). Both will keep well in the refrigerator for a few days and can be easily tossed together to make a salad for a quick meal.**

2 cups Quinoa or Couscous with Fennel (page 310)
1 cup Basic Roasted Vegetables (page 256)
1 cup flat-leaf parsley leaves, roughly chopped
¼ cup extra-virgin olive oil
3 tablespoons apple cider vinegar
1 tablespoon Dijon mustard (optional)
Kosher salt and freshly ground black pepper

In a large bowl, toss all of the ingredients to combine. Serve the salad chilled or at room temperature.

**Serves 4**

# Cold Sesame Noodles





**This is a lunch-box favorite. Keep it simple or add some of veggies and protein: strips of bell pepper, broccoli florets, or cooked peas, or cooked edamame or shredded left-over chicken.**

6 tablespoons peanut butter or tahini
¼ cup hot water
2 tablespoons sesame oil
¼ cup low-sodium soy sauce
½ teaspoon ground ginger
1 garlic clove, minced
8 ounces soba noodles or other thin pasta, cooked
2 to 3 tablespoons minced scallions or chives
½ cup bean sprouts (optional)

1. In a small bowl, whisk together the peanut butter or tahini, hot water, sesame oil, soy sauce, ground ginger, and garlic until they form a smooth paste.
2. In a large bowl, toss the noodles with the paste, the scallions, and the bean sprouts, if using.
3. Refrigerate. Pack in a thermos for lunch and eat with chopsticks!

**Serves 4**

# Rice Noodle Salad

**Substitute tamarind sauce for the soy sauce to make a nice, gluten-free alternative to wheat-noodle dishes. The cabbage gives it a bit of crunch and the flavors are simple but fresh. You can prepare the dressing and vegetables up to a day in advance and refrigerate. When ready to serve, continue with Steps 2 and 3.**

### Dressing

½ cup freshly squeezed lime juice
3 tablespoons low-sodium soy sauce
2 teaspoons sugar
2 to 3 teaspoons peeled and grated fresh ginger
½ teaspoon red pepper flakes, or a pinch of cayenne (optional)
¼ cup sesame oil
¼ cup canola oil

### Salad

6 to 8 ounces dried vermicelli or thin rice noodles
2 cups thinly sliced napa cabbage or bok choy
3 scallions, thinly sliced on the diagonal
1 cup coarsely chopped fresh cilantro
1 medium carrot, grated or cut into fine julienne
¼ cup peanuts, toasted and crushed

1 Mix together the ingredients for the dressing. Taste and adjust the seasonings.

2 Cook the noodles according to the package instructions, or soak in hot water for 10 to 20 minutes until tender. Drain well and chop coarsely.

3 In a bowl, toss the noodles with half of the dressing and all of the vegetables. Add the remaining dressing, as needed, and toss well. Top with the peanuts. Serve the salad cold or at room temperature.

**Serves 4 to 6**

# Vegetarian Brown Rice Sushi





**Alice's youngest daughter, Phoebe, came back from a play date once, excited that she made sushi with her young friend. Never mind that she's part Japanese by heritage, Phoebe was never excited about sushi until she made it herself. Do the prep for the rice, and let kids fill with colorful vegetables, roll, and cut their own creations.**

2 cups short-grain brown rice
¼ cup seasoned rice vinegar
2 tablespoons low-sodium soy sauce
Four 7 x 8-inch sheets sushi nori (toasted seaweed)
1 firm but ripe avocado
½ cucumber, peeled, seeded, and cut into matchsticks
1 carrot, cut into matchsticks
Soy sauce for dipping
Bamboo sushi mat (see Note)

1 Wash the rice under cold running water until the water runs clear. Drain well. In a saucepan, combine the rice and 2¾ cups water. Bring to a boil, reduce to a simmer, cover, and cook 35 to 40, minutes until the water is absorbed. Stir together the rice vinegar and soy sauce and mix into the rice. Mix thoroughly to combine the seasonings and to cause the rice to release its starch and become sticky. Cover and let cool completely. If made ahead, cover the rice, but keep at room temperature; do not refrigerate.

2 Place a sushi mat on a work surface with the slats running horizontally. Arrange a sheet of nori, shiny side down, on the mat. Using damp fingers, gently press one-fourth of the rice onto the nori in a layer, leaving a 2-inch border on the side farthest from you.

3 Halve, pit, and thinly slice the avocado. Arrange one-fourth of the cucumber, carrot, and avocado in rows across the middle of the rice.

4 Lift the mat up with your thumbs, holding the filling in place with your fingers, and fold the mat over the filling so that the upper and lower edges of the rice meet. Then squeeze gently but firmly along the length of the roll. The nori border will still be flat on the mat. Open the mat and roll the sushi log forward to seal with the nori border. Transfer the roll to a cutting board. Make 3 more logs in the same manner with the remaining ingredients, then, using a slightly wet knife, cut each log crosswise into 6 or 8 pieces. Serve with soy sauce for dipping.

**Serves 4**

Note: If you do not have a sushi mat, cut the nori sheet in half, fill with the rice and vegetables, and roll into a cone shape for hand-rolled sushi.

**Ideas** Other fillings to keep in mind: leftover Broiled Salmon (page 216), cooked shrimp, strips of omelet-style egg, steamed, sliced mushrooms, or dark leafy greens.

# Mini Pizzas



**These alternatives to "genuine" pizza really deliver. You can prepare a batch and freeze individually. Then you or your kids can grab a few and heat them up in a toaster oven for a quick lunch or snack anytime.**

1. Start with English muffins halves, sliced bagels, a small baguette, pita halves, or tortillas.
2. Spread on tomato or marinara sauce, pesto, or tapenade.
3. Add shredded cheddar, Monterey Jack, or mozzarella cheese, or try goat cheese, ricotta, or feta.
4. Top with sliced mushrooms, pitted olives, bell peppers, zucchini, scallions, corn kernels, tomato slices, fresh basil leaves, spinach, broccoli, eggplant, artichoke hearts, or left-over or cured meats.
5. Heat in the toaster oven or broiler until the cheese has melted.

# Pinwheel Pleasures

**Mini sandwiches are easy to make and ideal for lunches, snacks, or party hors d'oeuvre.**

Trim the crusts off a slice of bread and flatten the bread with a rolling pin. Top with a thin layer of filling and roll up. Seal with a dab of butter, or skewer with a toothpick. Cut into thin rounds.

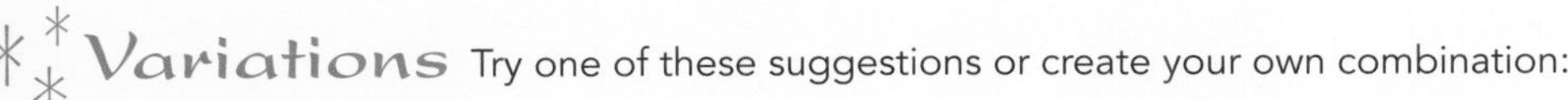

**Variations** Try one of these suggestions or create your own combination:

- Whole wheat bread with egg salad.
- Rye bread with peanut butter and jam.
- Sourdough bread with smoked salmon and cream cheese.
- Raisin bread with cottage cheese and mashed avocado.
- Sprouted wheat bread with tuna salad.
- Oat nut bread with hummus and alfalfa sprouts.
- Pumpernickel bread with spinach, turkey, and mayonnaise.

# Mini Ham and Pea Quiches

**Mini quiches are perfect, savory little handfuls. See the freezing tip on the following page so these are always on hand!**

1½ cups all-purpose flour
¼ teaspoon salt
8 tablespoons (1 stick) unsalted butter, at room temperature
¼ cup ice-cold water
1 cup diced ham or left-over chicken
One 10-ounce bag frozen baby peas, thawed
6 large eggs, lightly beaten
¼ cup whole milk, or substitute a bit of cream, if desired
1 cup shredded hard cheese, such as Swiss or Gruyère

1 Preheat the oven to 425°F.

2 In a bowl, mix together the flour and salt. Cut and work the butter into the flour until pea-size pieces form. Add the ice-cold water and mix with a fork until the ingredients are blended completely and a dough forms.

3 Divide the dough into quarters and then cut each piece into thirds. On a lightly floured work surface, roll out each piece of dough very thinly into 6-inch circles.

4 Grease the cups of a standard 12-cup muffin pan and insert a dough circle into each cup, creasing the dough as needed to fit. Bake the quiche shells for 8 minutes. Set the shells aside to cool.

5 In a separate bowl, mix together the ham, peas, eggs, milk, and cheese. Fill each quiche shell with the egg mixture. Bake for 20 to 25 minutes, until the edges of the shells are lightly brown and the egg is set. Let cool slightly before serving.

**Makes 12 muffin-size quiches**

## Variation

**Mini Frittatas:** In a bowl, mix together the ham, peas, eggs, and milk. Grease the cups of a standard 12-cup muffin pan with a bit of butter. Divide the cheese evenly among the muffin cups; this will form a cheesy crust. Divide the filling mixture evenly among the cups. Follow the baking instructions in Step 3. See Tip below for freezing instructions. See also Kitchen Sink Frittatas (page 67) for more filling ideas. Mini frittatas are also great when made in mini muffin pans for really little bites!

## Tips

To freeze mini quiche shells, follow Step 2 and let cool. Remove from the pans and freeze in a single layer until solid. Transfer the shells to an airtight freezer container. Frozen shells are handy to use up leftover meats or vegetables. Just fill one or two with a bit of egg mixture and some left-over tidbits and bake in a toaster oven at 425°F for 15 to 20 minutes.

To freeze mini quiches or frittatas, cool on a wire rack and freeze in a single layer until solid. Wrap individually in plastic wrap and store in the freezer to grab for breakfast or for an after-school snack. To reheat, bake in a toaster oven at 350°F for about 20 minutes.

# Mushroom Tart

**Mushrooms are a good source of vitamins and minerals and have a long history of medicinal use in Asian cultures. Sauté them in a bit of olive oil with garlic or shallots for a side dish, or use as a topping for this delicious savory tart. This recipe is a reminder of just how quickly frozen puff pastry can be turned into a snack, appetizer, or light meal.**

1 pound mixed fresh mushrooms
2 tablespoons olive oil
2 garlic cloves, minced
Kosher salt and freshly ground black pepper
1 sheet frozen puff pastry, thawed
1 large egg, beaten with 1 tablespoon water
½ cup grated Fontina or Gouda cheese

1 Wash, trim, and slice the mushrooms ¼ inch thick. Heat the oil in a cast-iron skillet over medium heat. Add the mushrooms, garlic, and a pinch of salt and cook, stirring, until the mushrooms have released their moisture and have started to brown, about 10 minutes. Season to taste with salt and pepper.

2 Preheat the oven to 425°F.

3 Unroll the puff pastry onto a baking sheet lined with parchment paper. Prick the center of the pastry all over with the tines of a fork, leaving a 1-inch border on the edges. Brush the pastry with the egg wash and bake for about 5 minutes until the pastry begins to puff. Remove from the oven and let rest 5 minutes.

4 Scatter the mushrooms over the pastry, leaving the border uncovered.

5 Bake the tart until golden brown, about 10 minutes. Scatter the cheese over the mushrooms and bake a few minutes more until the cheese has melted. Let cool slightly on a wire rack before slicing and serving.

**Serves 4 to 8**

## Variations

**Vegetable Tart:** Use ½ pound fresh mushrooms and sauté with ½ pound sliced dark leafy greens or red bell pepper strips.

**Roasted Asparagus Tart:** This makes a pretty presentation, and a thin bed of cream makes it a bit more decadent. Toss 1 pound asparagus spears with 2 tablespoons olive oil. Roast in a single layer on a baking sheet in a 450°F oven for 10 to 15 minutes. In a small saucepan, reduce ½ cup heavy cream by half, stirring constantly. Set aside to cool. Follow Step 3 of the recipe for the puff pastry. Spread the cooled cream over the pastry, leaving the border uncovered. Top with the asparagus spears, season to taste with salt and pepper, and continue with Step 5.

# Sausage and Pepper Empanadas

**Making empanadas is a fun activity to do with kids. Here, the dough is quick and easy, and pliable to work with. Make a batch or two for the freezer so you can just pull out a couple to heat up for snacks, breakfast, or a small meal anytime.**

1 tablespoon canola oil
1 pound favorite sausage
½ cup diced onion
1 cup diced red bell pepper
1 jalapeño pepper, seeded and diced (optional)
1 cup tomato sauce
Kosher salt or freshly ground black pepper
One 8-ounce package shredded mixed cheese blend
2½ cups all-purpose flour
1 teaspoon sugar
1 teaspoon salt
8 tablespoons (1 stick) unsalted butter, at room temperature
½ cup milk
1 egg

1 Heat the oil in a medium frying pan over medium heat. Remove the sausage meat from its casing and sauté it until brown, breaking it apart with a spatula as you cook it. Remove the meat with a slotted spoon and set aside.

2 Add the onion, bell pepper, and jalapeño to the pan and cook until soft, stirring occasionally, about 5 minutes. Return the sausage to the pan, add the tomato sauce, season with salt and black pepper to taste, and simmer for about 15 minutes. Remove from the heat, mix in the shredded cheese, and set aside or refrigerate until ready to use.

3 In a bowl, mix together the flour, sugar, and 1 teaspoon salt. Cut and work the butter into the flour until pea-size pieces form. Add the milk and egg, and mix until the ingredients are blended and a dough forms.

4 Divide the dough into quarters and then divide each quarter into 5 or 6 pieces for a total of 20 to 24 pieces. On a lightly floured work surface, roll each piece into a ball and flatten, with the plam of your hand, into a 4-inch circle.

5 Lightly brush the rim of each circle with a bit of water. Place 1 heaping tablespoon of the sausage mixture in the center of each circle. Fold the dough over the filling, pressing the edges with a fork to seal. Repeat with the remaining circles and sausage mixture. (At this point, the empanadas can be frozen in a single layer on a baking sheet for about 1 hour until firm. When frozen solid, transfer to gallon-size, plastic freezer bags and freeze for up to 1 month.)

6 Preheat the oven to 400°F. Lightly grease a baking sheet. Arrange the empanadas on the prepared baking sheet. Bake for 15 to 20 minutes, until golden and warmed through. Transfer to wire racks to cool slightly. Serve warm.

**Makes 20 to 24 small empanadas**



**Variations** Practically anything goes for empanada fillings: sweet or savory; vegetarian; meat or seafood; cheesy or dairy-free. Here are some combinations:

- Canned beans, jarred salsa, and cheese.
- Roasted vegetables (page 256) and goat cheese.
- Sautéed mushrooms and goat cheese.
- Potatoes, hard-boiled eggs, and raisins.
- Turkey-veggie mixture (page 237) and cheese.
- Shrimp, red bell peppers, cheese, and tomato sauce.
- Fruit and cheese fillings for breakfast empanadas.
- Fruit fillings for dessert empanadas.

**Tip** Try using frozen puff pastry dough for a quick, flaky crust. Cut the dough into squares to make triangular empanadas.

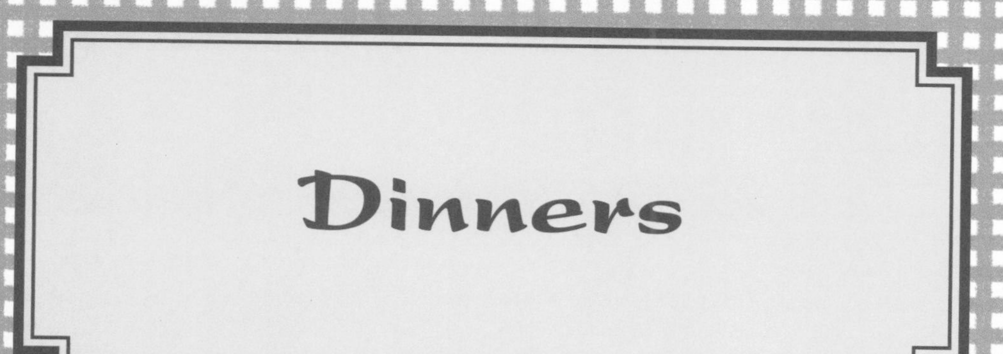

# Dinners

# Rice and Beans



**The nutritional benefits of beans are undisputed, but that is secondary to how delicious and, indeed, comforting they can be. Serve these rice and beans with some grated cheese and tomato salsa, and a big bowl of leafy green vegetables, and you have the makings of a very satisfying meal.**

1 pound dried black, red kidney, or pinto beans
1 bay leaf
Kosher salt
3 tablespoons olive oil
1 large Spanish onion, chopped
4 garlic cloves, minced
1 large red or green bell pepper, cored, seeded, and diced
3 cups cooked brown rice
1 cup chicken, beef, or vegetable broth
1 to 2 tablespoons balsamic vinegar

1 Rinse the beans, put them into a large pot, and add water to cover by a few inches. Bring to a boil, then turn off the heat and let the beans soak for 1 hour. (Alternatively, you may wish to soak the beans overnight.)

2 Drain the beans, return them to the pot, and cover again with plenty of fresh water. Add the bay leaf and simmer over low heat until tender. This may take anywhere from 1 to 2 hours, depending on the age of the beans. When the beans have softened but are not completely cooked, add up to 2 teaspoons of salt to taste. The beans will become as salty as the water they are cooked in. Do not add salt at the beginning of the cooking process—it will prevent the beans from cooking through. Continue to cook until the beans are tender.

3 Heat the olive oil in a medium frying pan over medium heat. Add the onion, garlic, and bell pepper and sauté until soft and the onion is translucent, about 10 minutes.

4 Drain the beans of most of their liquid. Remove and discard the bay leaf. Add the sautéed onion, garlic, and bell pepper, the cooked rice, and the broth to the pot. Simmer for 10 to 15 minutes, stirring occasionally, to blend the flavors and to achieve the consistency you like. Just before serving, stir in the vinegar to taste.

**Serves 6**

## Variations

- Add additional seasonings such as cumin and oregano for Mexican-style beans.
- Add a smoked ham hock to the beans when cooking, then shred the meat and add it to the beans when they're done.
- Add fresh, sautéed, or canned poblano chiles in place of the bell pepper.
- Add a pinch of saffron to the rice while it's cooking, and a splash of sherry to the beans as they simmer for a Spanish accent.

# Macaroni and Cheese





**We know you are addicted to the stuff in the box, but try this and we promise, you'll never go back. We have made it for parties and never had any left over. It takes a little bit of work to make the white sauce that serves as the base for this recipe, but it is well worth the effort. We once made this recipe with really expensive cheese that we hand grated, which was a bit messy and time-consuming. The next time, we used a bag of inexpensive preshredded cheese, which took no time at all. Both versions tasted the same.**

1 pound elbow macaroni
4 tablespoons (½ stick) unsalted butter
¼ cup all-purpose flour
3 cups whole milk
¾ cup heavy cream
1 pound shredded cheddar or Monterey Jack cheese
4 teaspoons Dijon mustard
1½ teaspoons kosher salt
Freshly ground black pepper
3 cups packaged croutons, any flavor you like
2 tablespoons unsalted butter, melted
4 ounces shredded cheddar cheese

1 Preheat the oven to 400°F. Butter a 13 x 9-inch casserole dish.

2 Cook the macaroni in a large pot of boiling salted water until it's tender but still a bit firm in the middle—al dente. Reserve 1 cup of the cooking water, drain the pasta, and transfer it to a large bowl.

3 While the pasta is cooking, melt the butter in a heavy pot over low heat.

4 Whisk in the flour and cook, continuing to whisk, for about 5 minutes. Whisk in a few tablespoonfuls of the milk to ensure that lumps don't form, then whisk in the remaining milk in a slow, steady stream. Bring to a boil, whisking the whole time. When the sauce starts to boil, reduce the heat to a simmer and continue whisking for 2 minutes more.

5 Stir in the cream, 1 pound shredded cheese, mustard, salt, and pepper to taste. Remove the sauce from the heat and pour it over the macaroni in the bowl. Add the cup of reserved cooking water, mix, and transfer to the prepared baking dish; the mixture will be runny—not to worry!

6 Make the topping: Crush the croutons while still in the bag and empty the crumbs into a bowl. Add the melted butter and 4 ounces cheese and mix to combine.

7 Sprinkle the topping over the macaroni and cheese in the casserole dish and bake for about 30 minutes, or until bubbling and browned on top. Serve hot.

**Serves 6 to 8**

(See the next page for Variations)

## Variations

**Top with tomato:** Blanch, peel, and cut 2 ripe tomatoes into ½-inch-thick slices. Top the macaroni with the tomato slices at the end of Step 5 and season with salt and pepper to taste. Continue with the remaining steps.

**Add roasted broccoli:** Toss 3 cups broccoli florets with a bit of olive oil and roast on a baking sheet in the 400°F oven for 30 minutes while you prepare the macaroni and cheese. Add the roasted broccoli at the end of Step 5 and continue with the remaining steps.

**Add meat:** Add 1 pound browned hamburger meat or a bit of crumbled crispy bacon to the pasta and sauce mixture before you add the topping.

**Add peas:** Add a bag of frozen peas to the pasta-and-sauce mixture before you add the topping.

**Make Macaroni Pie:** This dish is essentially a macaroni-and-cheese casserole, most popular in the southern United States, Jamaica, Trinidad, and the Caribbean. This moist pie with pockets of melted cheese couldn't be simpler to throw together. Preheat the oven to 350°F. Grease a 13 x 9-inch baking dish and add 1 pound cooked and drained elbow macaroni. Mix in 1 pound cheddar cheese cubes (make sure some of the cheese stays on the top) and pour in about 4 cups whole milk. Bake about 45 minutes, or longer for a crispier top. Let cool 5 minutes before serving. Serves 6 to 8.

# Risotto with Zucchini and Peas

**Just say "risotto" and your mouth waters and your shoulders relax. Lucky are the kids whose mother will stand over the pot and stir for a half hour to make this favorite comfort food!**

3½ cups chicken broth or stock, preferably homemade (Basic Chicken Stock, page 98)
3 tablespoons unsalted butter
1 pound zucchini, peeled and cut into ½-inch chunks
Kosher salt and freshly ground black pepper
½ cup finely chopped onion
1½ cups Arborio rice
½ cup dry white wine
1 cup frozen peas, thawed
½ cup grated Parmesan cheese

1 Heat the broth or stock and 2½ cups water in a small saucepan over low heat. Keep warm.

2 Melt 2 tablespoons of the butter in a large saucepan over medium heat. Add the zucchini and season with salt and pepper to taste. Cook, stirring often, until golden brown, about 10 minutes. Remove the zucchini from the pan and set aside.

3 Add the onion to the pan and cook until soft, about 5 minutes. Season with salt and pepper to taste. Add the rice and cook, stirring, until the edges are translucent, about 3 minutes. Add the wine and cook until absorbed, about 2 minutes.

4 Continue to cook and stir, adding a cup of broth and waiting until the liquid has been completely absorbed before adding the remaining broth, ¼ cup at a time. Cook, stirring constantly, until the rice is tender, about 30 minutes. Add the zucchini and peas and cook for about 2 minutes, until the peas are bright green. Remove the risotto from the heat and stir in the remaining 1 tablespoon butter and the grated cheese. Serve immediately.

**Serves 4 to 6**

**Butternut Squash Risotto:** Substitute 1 pound diced butternut squash for the zucchini. Replace the wine with additional chicken broth. Garnish with crispy, crumbled bacon for an extra treat.

# Buying Organic

## MEAT AND ANIMAL PRODUCTS

**If you choose to make meat and other animal products part of your diet, you should know what you're getting, whether your favorite dish is pork tenderloin, leg of lamb, rotisserie chicken, filet mignon, turkey burgers, meat loaf, or macaroni and cheese. So far, government studies have found no appreciable difference in the nutrient content of traditional vs. organic foods, but many believe that animals that are raised in fresh air in clean surroundings and brought to market humanely—without loads of antibiotics and hormones—are happier, healthier, and often ... well, tastier. Looking to justify the added expense of organics? There are numerous reasons to switch.**

### DOUBLE WHAMMY

Not only do we get unwanted chemicals given directly to traditionally farmed animals, but the animals themselves are fed grain farmed with pesticides, herbicides, fungicides, and fertilizers, which are stored as toxins in their fat, which we eat. All farming was organic until the twentieth century, when the addition of synthetic chemicals set off the reactive movement called the Green Revolution, in the 1940s. Ahead of its time, the movement helped to raise society's awareness, so that today we know that consuming unneeded antibiotics and hormones is undesirable in general, and it is especially suggested that children, pregnant women, and cancer survivors may benefit from avoiding these substances in animal products.

## GREENING THE EARTH

When you buy organic meat and poultry you are doing the planet a good turn, too. In the United States, "certified organic production" is defined as a system that "fosters cycling of resources, promotes ecological balance, and conserves biodiversity." Organic farming practices are designed to benefit the environment by reducing pollution, conserving water, and preserving soil quality, and livestock raised this way must eat nothing but certified organic plant material themselves.

## WORST OFFENDERS

Want to start buying organic animal products on a limited budget? Begin with poultry, eggs, and pork. Conventionally raised birds are often kept in very crowded, often unsanitary buildings day and night. Between the poor-quality food, lack of exercise, and close quarters, sickness spreads like wildfire through the barns. Sows are kept in pens so small they cannot turn around, and pork from these large factory farms can be tough and flavorless, a far cry from the era when pork was rich, juicy, and consumed in moderation.

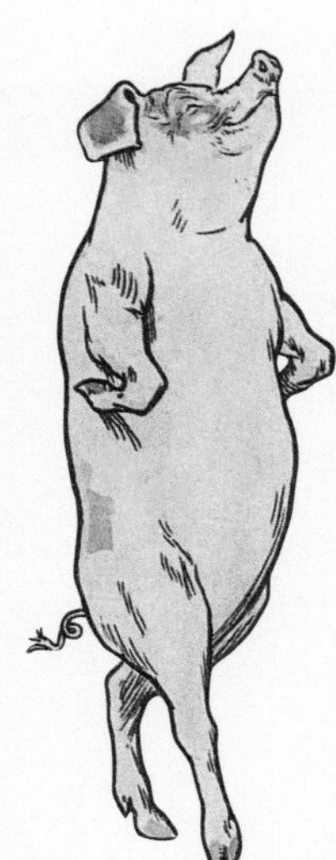

## LEARN MORE

The USDA has a wealth of information on the certification and perceived quality of organic versus traditional animal products. Go to www.usda.gov.

# Southwestern Chicken Tacos



**Tacos make a fun dinner, and for picky eaters who like to play with their food, stuffing their own tortilla shells is ideal. Traditional tacos often feature shredded or ground beef spiced up with taco seasoning, topped with shredded cheese, tomatoes, lettuce, olives, guacamole, and sour cream. The following regional variations may be off the beaten path for many taco lovers, but once you try them, they may become the new standard at your dinner table.**

1 tablespoon olive oil
12 ounces boneless, skinless chicken breasts, cut into small pieces
1 cup favorite salsa
½ cup fresh or frozen corn kernels
½ cup finely chopped red and green bell peppers
½ cup canned black beans, rinsed and drained
8 taco shells
1½ cups shredded lettuce
½ cup shredded cheddar cheese or Mexican white cheese
1 tomato, chopped
Sour cream

1. Heat the olive oil in a large frying pan over medium heat. Add the chicken and ½ cup of the salsa, and cook for about 5 minutes, stirring frequently, until the chicken is cooked through.
2. Stir in the corn kernels and chopped bell peppers and cook for about 3 minutes. Add the beans and cook until the mixture has reduced slightly, about 5 minutes.
3. Serve the chicken mixture in a bowl accompanied by the taco shells, lettuce, cheese, tomato, the remaining ½ cup salsa, and the sour cream.

**Serves 8**



## Variations

**Tacos with Homemade Salsa:** Homemade salsa is simple to make and tastes so much fresher than jarred. Simply core and chop 3 large ripe tomatoes and mix in a bowl with ½ cup chopped red onion, ¼ cup finely chopped fresh cilantro, and, if you want a little heat, 1 or 2 jalapeño peppers, seeds and membranes removed and discarded, finely chopped. Add ¼ cup freshly squeezed lime juice and sea salt to taste. Makes about 2 cups salsa.

**Veggie Tacos:** Heat 1 tablespoon olive oil in a large frying pan over medium heat. Sauté ½ cup thinly sliced onion and 1 cup thinly sliced bell peppers for about 5 minutes until tender. Add 1 cup thinly sliced zucchini and cook for about 5 minutes more. Add ¼ cup water and 1 minced garlic clove. Bring the mixture to a simmer. Add 2½ cups canned, low-sodium refried black beans and ¼ cup water. Bring the mixture to a boil. When the mixture is heated through and has reached the desired consistency, remove from heat and stir in ¾ cup chopped tomato. Serve the veggie mixture in a bowl accompanied by taco shells, shredded lettuce, shredded cheese, and sour cream. Serves 8.

# Sizzling Fajitas

**An easy way to turn dinnertime into fiesta time is by dishing up this sizzling serve-yourself meal. Keep the tortillas warm by covering them with a cloth napkin. If you have finicky eaters in your family, this meal lets them customize to their hearts' content.**

1 tablespoon olive oil
1½ pounds skirt or flank steak, cut into diagonal 2-inch strips
2 yellow or white onions, peeled and sliced into strips
1 red bell pepper, cored, seeded, and cut into 2-inch strips
1 green bell pepper, cored, seeded, and cut into 2-inch strips
1 yellow bell pepper, cored, seeded, and cut into 2-inch strips
Eight 8-inch flour tortillas
Guacamole (page 146)
Homemade Salsa (page 191)
Sour cream
½ head romaine lettuce, shredded
2 tomatoes, sliced
½ red onion, chopped

1 Heat the oil in a large cast-iron skillet over medium-high heat. Then add the steak strips and cook on both sides, about 6 minutes total.

2 Remove the meat from the skillet. Add the onions and bell peppers to the skillet and sauté until soft, about 10 minutes. Combine with the meat.

3 Warm the tortillas in a clean skillet and serve immediately with the guacamole, salsa, sour cream, shredded lettuce, sliced tomatoes, and chopped onion.

**Serves 4**

## Variations

**Shrimp or Chicken Fajitas:** Substitute peeled and deveined shrimp or strips of boneless, skinless chicken breasts for the steak. Reduce the cooking time for the shrimp to about 5 minutes total. Increase the cooking time slightly for the chicken to about 10 minutes total.

**Vegetarian Fajitas:** Substitute 2-inch strips of zucchini and carrots for the steak and sauté the veggies with the onions and bell peppers in Step 2.

# One-Dish Stir-fry



**Every once in a while Alice simply stir-fries up lots of ingredients to make a one-dish meal to serve with rice. It's not the most elegant dish, but with kids it works. You can add tofu for those who don't want as much meat, and two or three types of vegetables. Always include a vegetable you know your kids will eat and a vegetable you are trying to get them used to.**

**Marinade**

2 teaspoons low-sodium soy sauce
2 teaspoons cornstarch
2 teaspoons dry sherry
2 teaspoons water
¾ pound boneless, skinless chicken breasts, sliced, or boneless lean beef, sliced
1½ teaspoons peanut oil

**Cooking Sauce**

½ cup water or chicken broth
1 tablespoon dry sherry
2 tablespoons low-sodium soy sauce or oyster sauce
¼ teaspoon sugar
1 teaspoon sesame oil
1 tablespoon cornstarch

**Stir-fry**

2½ tablespoons peanut oil
1 garlic clove, smashed or minced
1 pound vegetables: broccoli (blanched); asparagus (ends snapped off); red or green bell pepper (cored, seeded), and/or onion (peeled), cut into bite-size pieces; and, if available, canned straw mushrooms, water chestnuts (sliced), and/or baby corn
1 cup tofu cubes, drained (optional)

1 In a bowl, blend together the soy sauce, cornstarch, sherry, and water. Add the meat and stir to combine. Stir in the peanut oil. Set aside to marinate for 15 minutes.

2 In a bowl, mix together all of the ingredients for the cooking sauce. Set aside.

3 Heat a wok or large frying pan over high heat. When the pan is hot, add 1½ tablespoons of the peanut oil. When the oil begins to shimmer, add the garlic and stir. Add the meat and stir-fry until the chicken is opaque, 3 to 4 minutes, or until the beef is no longer pink, about 1½ minutes. Remove from the wok.

4 Clean the wok and wipe dry. Add the remaining 1 tablespoon peanut oil to the wok. When the oil is hot, add the vegetables and tofu, if using, and stir-fry for 30 seconds. Add 3 tablespoons water, cover, and cook for about 2 minutes for crisp vegetables, a bit longer for tender vegetables.

5 Return the meat to the wok. Stir the cooking sauce, add to the wok, and cook, stirring, until the sauce bubbles and thickens. If the sauce is thinner than you'd like, mix 1 teaspoon of cornstarch with 1 tablespoon of water until dissolved, stir in, and cook until thickened. Serve the stir-fry immediately.

**Serves 4**

(See the next page for **Variations**)

# Variations



**Pan-fried Noodles:** Prepare One-Dish Stir-fry without the tofu and increase the the water or broth in the cooking sauce to 1 cup. Set aside in a warm oven. Cook 1 pound thin egg noodles in a pot of boiling water according to package directions. Drain and toss with 1 teaspoon of seseame oil. Heat 1 tablespoon peanut oil in a large frying pan or wok over medium heat and spread the noodles evenly in the pan. Cook, without stirring, until noodles are browned on the bottom, about 5 minutes. Flip and brown the other side. Transfer to a large bowl and top with the meat-vegetable mixture. Serves 4.

**Basic Stir-fried Vegetables:** Clean, crisp vegetables, with nothing beyond a hint of oil, garlic, and ginger are the perfect accompaniment to main dishes with robust flavors. Heat a wok or wide frying pan over high heat. Add 2 tablespoons canola or peanut oil and let heat for 30 seconds. Add ½ teaspoon minced ginger and 1 minced garlic clove and stir. Add 1 pound cut vegetables (see below) and stir-fry for 1½ minutes. Add ½ teaspoon kosher salt and 1 to 3 tablespoons water or broth as indicated below. Cover and cook until the vegetables are crisp tender. Uncover, taste, and stir fry longer if you like the vegetables more tender, adding a bit more liquid if needed. Serve immediately. Serves 4.

Asparagus (¼-inch diagonal slices)/Zucchini (¼-inch slices): 2 tablespoons of liquid; cook covered for 2 to 3 minutes.

Bell Peppers (¼-inch slices): 1 tablespoon of liquid, cook covered for 1 minute.

Broccoli (bite-size pieces)/Cauliflower (bite-size pieces): 3 tablespoons of liquid; cook covered for 3 to 4 minutes.

Cabbage/Kale/Spinach/Chard (2-inch-wide strips): 1 tablespoon of liquid; cook covered for 2 minutes.

Carrot (¼-inch slices)/Celery (¼-inch slices)/Green Beans (1-inch pieces): 3 tablespoons of liquid; cook covered for 3 to 4 minutes.

Eggplant (1-inch cubes): 4 tablespoons of liquid; cook covered for 5 to 6 minutes.

Mushrooms (¼-inch slices)/Snow Peas (remove ends and string): 1 tablespoon of liquid; stir-fry 2 minutes.

# Stir-fried Tofu with Chicken and Peas

**This recipe and its variation are easy to make and perfect for even young children on solids. The stir-fried tofu can be spiced up with chili paste for adult tastes after the kids' portion has been removed from the pan. Serve these tofu dishes with rice and a vegetable. If you stir-fry a vegetable, you can do it while the tofu is steaming or after the stir-fried tofu is done and in a warm oven. An even easier accompaniment is Chinese Greens with Oyster Sauce (page 288).**

1 teaspoon low-sodium soy sauce
1 teaspoon dry sherry
1 teaspoon hoisin sauce (optional)
½ pound ground chicken or pork
3 tablespoons peanut oil
One 14-ounce package soft tofu
2 garlic cloves, minced
1 cup frozen peas
¾ cup chicken broth
2 tablespoons cornstarch
1½ teaspoons hot bean sauce or chili paste (optional)

1. In a bowl, blend together the soy sauce, sherry, and hoisin sauce, if using. Add the meat and stir to combine. Stir in 1 tablespoon of the oil. Set aside.
2. Cut the tofu into ½-inch cubes and place in a colander to drain.
3. Heat a wok or large frying pan over high heat. When the wok is hot, add the remaining 2 tablespoons oil. When the oil begins to shimmer, add the garlic and stir-fry. Then add the meat and stir-fry until no longer pink, about 2 minutes. Add the drained tofu, peas, and broth and stir once or twice. Cover and cook for 3 minutes.
4. While the stir-fry is cooking, mix the cornstarch with ¼ cup of water.

5 Uncover the wok, add the cornstarch mixture down the side of the wok, and stir until the mixture bubbles and thickens, 1 to 2 minutes.

6 If desired, remove a portion for children before adding the hot bean sauce or chili paste to the adults' portion left in the wok. Stir well and let simmer for a minute or two. Remove from the wok and serve immediately or keep it warm in the oven.

**Serves 4**

**Tip** Adults may love spicy foods, but kids usually can't tolerate them as well. When you make this recipe, put two serving bowls of the tofu on the table—one spicy and one not. Children can serve themselves mostly from the nonspicy version and mix in as much from the spicy bowl as he/she wishes.

## Variation

**Steamed Tofu with Meat:** This is a simple comfort dish that Alice grew up with. Follow Step 1 in the previous recipe. Cut one 14-ounce package soft tofu into 8 pieces, approximately ¾ inch thick. Place the tofu in a shallow, heatproof dish or pie plate in one layer. (Alice usually manages to fit most of the tofu in a dish, angling some at the rim of the plate, if necessary. You can also do this in two batches, steaming the second batch while you eat the first.) Add a spoonful of the meat mixture to the top of each piece of tofu. Press down slightly with the back of a spoon. Place the heatproof dish or pie plate on a rack in a wok or large frying pan with a few inches of boiling water, cover with a domed lid, and steam for 15 to 20 minutes. Serve with a bit of oyster sauce on the side. Serves 4.

# Chicken Fingers

**Kids adore these, and who can blame them? Crunchy on the outside, tender in the inside, and lots of fun dipping action. If you are using regular bread crumbs, try mixing in ¼ cup of wheat germ for a little nutrient boost. Prepare two batches of the chicken fingers and freeze the extra one to pull out for snacks and lunchboxes.**

⅓ cup honey
3 tablespoons Dijon mustard
2 tablespoons rice vinegar
4 boneless, skinless chicken breasts
1 large egg
3 tablespoons whole milk
¼ cup grated Parmesan cheese
1½ cups dry bread crumbs, preferably whole wheat or panko, unseasoned
Kosher salt and freshly ground black pepper
2 tablespoons unsalted butter
2 tablespoons canola oil

1 In a small bowl, mix together the honey, mustard, and rice vinegar. Cover and refrigerate until ready to serve.

2 Slice the chicken breasts into ½-inch strips. If you prefer nuggets, cut them into bite-size pieces.

3 In a bowl, whisk together the egg and milk. In a separate bowl, mix together the cheese, bread crumbs, and salt and pepper to taste.

4 Dip the chicken pieces in the egg mixture and then roll them in the bread crumbs. Place them in a single layer on two baking sheets lined with wax paper. You can freeze the chicken at this point, (see Tip).

5 Melt the butter and oil in a large cast-iron skillet over medium-high heat. Add the chicken and cook in batches to avoid overcrowding the skillet for about 15 minutes, turning the chicken strips as they brown. Transfer to paper towels to drain excess oil. Alternatively, you can bake the strips in the oven at 425°F for 15 to 20 minutes until crisp and golden brown, turning the pieces over halfway through. Serve the chicken fingers with the honey-mustard dipping sauce, or with one of the dips below.

**Serves 4 to 6**

**Tip** To freeze the chicken fingers, prepare the chicken according to Steps 1 through 4. Put the baking sheet in the freezer for about 1 hour, or until the strips are solid, then transfer them to a heavy-duty plastic bag for storing. To cook, thaw in the refrigerator overnight and continue with Step 5.

## Variations

**Bleu Cheese Dip/Dressing:** Mix together ¾ cup mayonnaise, ¾ cup sour cream, 5 ounces crumbled bleu cheese, 3 tablespoons freshly squeezed lemon juice, and 2 tablespoons sherry vinegar. Cover and refrigerate until ready to use. Makes about 2 cups.

**Thousand Island Dip/Dressing:** Mix together 1 cup mayonnaise, ⅓ cup ketchup, ¼ cup sweet pickle relish, and 1 tablespoon minced onion. Cover and refrigerate until ready to use. Makes about 1¾ cups.

**Russian Dip/Dressing:** Make the Thousand Island Dip/Dressing above and add ¼ cup chili sauce. Cover and refrigerate until ready to use. Makes about 2 cups.

**Asian Thousand Island Dip/Dressing:** Mix together 1 cup mayonnaise, ½ cup ketchup, ¼ cup sesame oil, 2 tablespoons each minced garlic and peeled and minced fresh ginger, and 2 tablespoons each fish sauce and lime juice. Cover and refrigerate until ready to use. Makes about 1¾ cups.

M.Vanasek

# Rotisserie Chicken

**Picking up a rotisserie chicken at the supermarket is not only a neat way to have dinner ready at a moment's notice, but roast chicken, shredded, diced, or chopped into large pieces, also forms the basis for an unlimited variety of super easy recipes that children can learn to make. Another thing: unlike beef, the fat on a chicken is separable from the skin, which makes it a good choice for a low-fat eating plan. Buying a rotisserie chicken is relatively economical—not much more than a raw chicken, plus no roasting pan to clean! Serve your cut-up cold rotisserie chicken on salads, in wraps, or add shredded chicken to soups, burritos, pizza, and pasta.**

**AT THE STORE:** The rotisserie chicken should be the last item you pick up before leaving for home. Make sure the bird is hot (above 140°F) or refrigerated to slow bacterial growth. Check the container for a good seal and place it in a plastic bag.

**AT HOME:** If not eating the hot chicken right away, cool the chicken slightly and remove the meat from the bones (shred, if desired), discard the skin, and store immediately in a covered container in the fridge for up to 4 days or in the freezer for up to 4 months.

**AT THE TABLE:** You can serve the hot roast chicken right away. Keep your chicken hot while you take a few minutes to heat up some sides or whip up a salad. On build-your-own-taco night, set out previously refrigerated shredded chicken along with shredded cheese, lettuce, chopped tomatoes, salsa, green chiles, and sour cream. Kids love tacos, and won't even notice if you serve low-fat dairy choices.

**IN THE FREEZER:** Since it goes well in so many recipes, you may want to keep some rotisserie chicken on hand at all times. For a family, purchase several birds at once and freeze in convenient-size portions (marked with the date). That way, you can simply move a frozen bag of shredded or chopped meat to the fridge in the morning (never thaw meat at room temperature), and it should be ready to use by evening.

## Ideas

**Soup:** 2 cups chicken for every 3 cans broth.

**Potpies:** 2 cups chicken for every 1 cup broth, ½ cup low-fat milk, and ½ cup each of cooked, diced potato, celery, carrots, and onion. Top with store-bought piecrusts. Bake at 375°F until the crust is golden, about 45 minutes.

**Pizza:** 1 cup chicken mixed with your other favorite toppings per single-serving whole-grain pizza crust. Even better: add some finely chopped spinach or lightly cooked broccoli.

**Chicken Salad:** See page 161.

**Meal in a Casserole:** Use 2 cups chicken for every 2 cups cooked rice, 1 can soup or broth, and about ½ cup each chopped mushrooms and two other raw veggie favorites. Bake at 325°F until the veggies are cooked, about 35 minutes.

# Chicken Paprika

**This is a yummy, lighter version of a traditional Hungarian comfort food that substitutes boneless, skinless chicken breast for the usual whole pieces and low-fat sour cream for full-fat sour cream (or you can try Greek-style yogurt). It is delicious and quick to make, and the family will gobble it up. The Variation, which follows, also uses quickly sautéed chicken breast strips, but the flavors satisfy different cravings.**

1 pound boneless, skinless chicken breasts, cut into 1-inch strips
2 tablespoons Hungarian sweet paprika
Kosher salt and freshly ground black pepper
1 tablespoon unsalted butter
1½ cups chopped onion
1 tablespoon olive oil
1 cup chopped tomatoes
¾ cup low-fat sour cream or Greek-style yogurt

1 Combine the chicken, 1 tablespoon of the paprika, and the salt and pepper in a bowl and toss to coat.

2 In a large sauté pan, melt the butter over medium-high heat. Add the chicken and sauté until cooked through, 5 to 8 minutes. Remove the chicken from the pan and set aside on a plate.

3 Add the onion and olive oil to the pan and sauté until tender, about 5 minutes. Add the remaining tablespoon paprika and stir well. Add the tomatoes and ½ **cup** water

and cook until the mixture is saucy, about 5 minutes. Return the chicken to the pan and cook until heated through. Remove the pan from the heat, add the sour cream to the pan, and stir until well combined. Serve immediately over rice or egg noodles.

**Serves 4**

## Variation

**Chicken with Ketchup:** Yes, ketchup, but this one is adapted from a *New York Times* recipe and it's sure to be a hit with any kid. Toss 1 pound boneless, skinless chicken breasts, cut into 1-inch strips, with ½ cup flour. Heat 2 tablespoons canola oil in a large nonstick frying pan over high heat. Add the chicken strips, season with salt and pepper, and sauté until cooked through. When one side has browned, turn the strips and cook the opposite side, 5 to 8 minutes total. Remove the chicken and set aside. Let the pan cool for a few minutes, then add another tablespoon canola oil and 2 tablespoons chopped garlic. Cook, stirring, for about 2 minutes. Add ¾ cup ketchup and cook until the mixture bubbles and darkens slightly. Return the chicken strips to the pan and coat with the sauce. Serve over steamed rice. Serves 4.

# Baked Chicken with Garlic and Shallots





**Alice's mother-in-law is a fabulous cook, and this is one of our favorite recipes from her. We love smashing up the melt-in-your-mouth garlic and shallots with a fork and smearing them over potatoes.**

- 3 tablespoons unsalted butter
- 6 medium shallots, halved and peeled
- 12 large garlic cloves, peeled
- 10 sprigs thyme, leaves picked
- 8 sprigs rosemary, needles picked
- 1 chicken, quartered, or 2 Cornish game hens, halved (3½ to 4 pounds)
- Kosher salt and freshly ground black pepper

1. Preheat the oven to 425°F.
2. Put the butter in a 15½ x 10½-inch glass baking dish. Put the dish in the oven while the oven is preheating.
3. When the butter has melted, remove the dish from the oven. Add the shallots, garlic, and herbs, and toss with the butter.
4. Dredge the chicken, skin side down, in the butter-herb mixture. Arrange the chicken, skin side up, in the dish, tuck the garlic and shallots underneath the chicken pieces, and season the chicken with salt and pepper to taste.
5. Bake until the chicken is browned and cooked through, 50 to 60 minutes, or slightly less if using Cornish game hens.

**Serves 4 to 6**

## Leftovers

**Easy Quesadillas:** Preheat the oven to 450°F. Place one flour or corn tortilla per person on a baking sheet and sprinkle each evenly with 2 tablespoons grated cheese and 2 tablespoons shredded left-over chicken. Add 1 tablespoon chopped spinach, bell peppers, or another favorite vegetable, if desired. Cover with another tortilla. Bake for 7 to 8 minutes until the edges are golden. Cut into quarters and serve hot with sour cream, guacamole, and/or salsa.

## Variations

**Add potatoes:** Use a larger roasting pan and add a dozen halved small potatoes, tossed with a bit of butter or olive oil, and spread them out to the edges of the pan.

**Add carrots:** Add 1 to 2 cups of baby carrots and another tablespoon of butter to the garlic and shallots in Step 3.

# Ultimate Roast Chicken

**This was Natasha's most favorite meal growing up. It is a recipe from her grandmother. Her mother made it often, and it is a staple in both her and her sister's cooking repertoires. They always serve this roast chicken with Swedish lingonberries in honor of their Swedish ancestry, but cranberry sauce works well, too. Sometimes they stuff it with doctored-up store-bought stuffing (see Variation) or serve it with mashed potatoes.**

One 4- to 5-pound roasting chicken, preferably organic
1 large lemon, peeled and cut in half
10 tablespoons (1 stick plus 2 tablespoons) unsalted butter
1 cup white wine
1 heaping tablespoon all-purpose flour

1 Preheat the oven to 425°F. Remove the liver and giblets from the cavity of the chicken. Rinse thoroughly and put them in a small saucepan. Cover with cold water and simmer for 1 hour.

2 Squeeze the lemon juice all over the chicken, including the cavity, leaving the lemon halves inside the cavity. Cut 8 tablespoons (1 stick) of the butter into thin slices. Put the slices all over the outside of the bird—like little solar panels.

3 Put the chicken into the oven. After 15 minutes, reduce the oven temperature to 350°F and baste the chicken with the melted butter from the bottom of the pan. Continue to baste every 15 minutes. When the chicken has been in the oven for 1 hour, add the white wine to the pan. Roast for another 30 minutes, basting once or twice, for a total of 1½ hours in the oven.

4 Meanwhile, remove the liver and giblets from the saucepan after they have simmered for 1 hour, and discard. Chill the broth so that you can easily skim the fat from the surface; the broth will be used to make the gravy.

5 Just before removing the chicken from the oven, melt the remaining 2 tablespoons butter in a saucepan over medium heat. Slowly whisk in the flour. As the mixture thickens, start adding some of the liver-giblet broth until you have a reasonable amount of gravy.

6 When the chicken has finished roasting, remove it from the oven and transfer it to a platter. Cover the chicken with aluminum foil and let it rest for a few minutes to allow the juices to redistribute. Pour off as much of the fat from the pan as you can, and add the remaining roasting juices to your gravy. Whisk to combine. Carve the chicken and serve.

**Serves 4**

## Variation

**Roast Chicken with Stuffing:** In a large frying pan, melt 2 tablespoons butter. Add ½ onion, chopped; 2 celery stalks, chopped; and/or ½ cup each chopped carrots, mushrooms, chestnuts; and a teaspoon each chopped fresh herbs of your choice (chives, sage, rosemary, thyme, oregano, and parsley all work here). Prepare 1 package of your favorite store-bought stuffing mix according to the package instructions, and mix in the sautéed veggies. Set the stuffing aside. Follow Steps 1 and 2 in the preceding recipe and stuff the bird in Step 2. Continue with the instructions, increasing the roasting time for the stuffed chicken to 2 to 2½ hours. Before carving the chicken, transfer the stuffing to a serving bowl. If you prefer, you can bake the stuffing in a separate baking dish alongside the chicken, basting occasionally with the chicken juices. Serves 4 to 6.

# Chicken Potpie





**Our friend Lenore is a grandmother and, truth be told, she probably should have her own cookbook altogether. She simply never makes anything that isn't high-end comfort food. Her chicken potpie is superb. She does make her own dough; however, to simplify life, we recommend you buy it frozen.**

3 cups chicken broth
3 poached and cubed boneless, skinless chicken breasts
4 to 5 cups cooked and cubed vegetables (any mixture of carrots, leeks, celery, mushrooms, pearl onions, zucchini, corn kernels, or green peas)
3 tablespoons unsalted butter
4 tablespoons all-purpose flour
½ cup heavy cream
Kosher salt and freshly ground black pepper
1 sheet frozen puff pastry, thawed
1 large egg, beaten

**1** Preheat the oven to 400°F.

**2** Boil the chicken broth until it has reduced by half. Set aside.

**3** Mix the chicken with the cubed vegetables and put in a 9-inch round casserole dish.

**4** In a saucepan, melt the butter, slowly whisk in the flour, and cook over medium-low heat for 2 to 3 minutes, whisking continuously. Add the broth and cream. Cook, whisking, until thickened, 3 to 4 minutes more. Season to taste with salt and pepper and pour over the chicken and vegetables in the casserole dish.

5 On a lightly floured work surface, roll out the dough to form the shape of your casserole dish, leaving an overlap of 1½ inches.

6 Brush the outside rim of the baking dish with some of the beaten egg. Place the pastry on top of the filling and crimp the overlap around the edges. Use a fork to tamp down the edges and give it a decorative look. Brush the beaten egg over the crust. Prick the dough all over with the tines of a fork to allow the steam to escape.

7 Bake the potpie for 20 minutes. Reduce the oven temperature to 375°F and bake for another 15 to 20 minutes.

**Serves 4 to 6**

# Know Your Fish

**Most of the calories in fish, like meat, poultry, dairy, and eggs, come from protein and fat. A 3-ounce portion of food from the protein group contains about 21 grams of protein. Fish and shellfish, with 0 to 9 grams of fat per portion, are one of the best low-calorie ways to get your daily allotment. But before you go on a fish binge, read further: there are other issues to be explored.**

## MERCURY

According to the FDA, the risk of mercury from eating healthy-size portions of most types of fish and shellfish is too low to be of concern for most adults. Some fish and shellfish, however, contain higher levels of mercury. The risk depends on the amounts consumed of these. The FDA advises women who may become pregnant, pregnant women, nursing mothers, and young children to avoid some types of fish and choose fish and shellfish that are lower in mercury:

- Avoid shark, swordfish, king mackerel, and tilefish.
- Eat two average meals (up to 12 ounces, less for young children) per week of varieties of fish or shellfish that are lower in mercury, such as canned light tuna, shrimp, salmon, catfish, and pollack. Limit canned albacore tuna and all tuna steaks to 6 ounces per week (it's higher in mercury than canned light tuna).
- If no local advisories are available, eat up to 6 ounces (one average meal) per week of fish you catch from local waters, but don't consume any other fish during that week.
- Fish sticks and "fast-food" sandwiches are commonly made from fish that are low in mercury.

## OTHER CONTAMINANTS

Many substances accumulate in the edible fatty tissues of fish. Concentrations vary considerably in individual fish of the same species, depending on factors such as their fat content, size, age, and gender, and whether they were caught in the open ocean or raised along the coastline. Older fish accumulate more toxins in general, but younger fish exposed to shore-side contaminants may have higher concentrations still.

## BOTTOM LINE

Fish and shellfish are an extremely nourishing component of a healthy diet. Benefits from eating fish far outweigh environmental concerns, as it takes long-term chronic exposure to excessive levels of contaminants to cause a problem. This means that even if you eat too much fish during one particular week nothing terrible will happen—just cut back the next week. It's the average over time that's important.

## LEARN MORE

Become an advocate for "ocean-friendly" seafood. Start with the Monterey Bay Aquarium Seafood Watch program's Super Green List, which includes seafood that meets criteria for low levels of contaminants, good omega-3 levels, and "greenness" (least likely to harm other species and the environment during harvesting). Visit www.montereybayaquarium.org.

# Broiled Salmon with Honey Dipping Sauce

**This is an easy meal that Alice makes regularly for her family. We also make it for our company holiday dinner for nonmeat eaters. Everyone loves it! You can serve it with just wedges of lemon, or try the dipping sauce below. Serve with Asparagus with Mustard Vinaigrette (page 260) and brown rice.**

4 salmon fillets (about 6 ounces each), skin on
Kosher salt

**Honey Dipping Sauce**
3 garlic cloves, minced
2 tablespoons minced cilantro
1 tablespoon sesame oil
2 tablespoons low-sodium soy sauce
1 tablespoon sherry (optional)
2 teaspoons rice or wine vinegar
1 tablespoon honey

1. Preheat the broiler.
2. In a bowl, mix together all the ingredients for the dipping sauce. Divide among four small bowls.
3. Arrange the fillets, skin side up in a broiling pan. Lightly sprinkle with salt.
4. Place the fillets under the broiler 4 inches from heat and broil for 4 minutes. Turn and cook another 3 minutes for a slightly pink interior. If you prefer your salmon cooked thoroughly, add a minute more on each side.
5. Serve immediately with the individual bowls of dipping sauce.

**Serves 4**

## Variations

**Oven-baked Salmon Rice Cakes:** Broil 2 extra salmon fillets with the preceding recipe, wrap, and reserve in the refrigerator for up to 2 days, or in the freezer until needed. Preheat the oven to 375°F. In a large bowl, flake the salmon and mix with ¼ cup finely chopped parsley, 2 tablespoons Parmesan cheese, 1 teaspoon Dijon mustard, 1 tablespoon mayonnaise, 2 beaten eggs, 1 cup cooked brown rice, a squeeze of lemon, and season with salt and pepper. Shape the mixture into eight 2-inch patties. Bake for about 20 minutes on an oiled baking sheet. Serve with Tartar Sauce (page 133) and lemon wedges, if desired. Serves 4.

**Pan-fried Salmon Rice Cakes:** Pulse 2 cups toasted rice cereal in a blender until fine and set aside in a bowl. Prepare and shape salmon patties per the instructions above. If the patties are too soft for dipping, place in the refrigerator or freezer for a few minutes. Beat 2 eggs in a bowl. Heat 2 tablespoons canola oil in a large cast-iron skillet. Dip the salmon patties in the egg, coat all sides with the rice cereal and place into the skillet. Fry the patties in batches, 3 to 4 minutes per side until golden brown. Serve with Tartar Sauce (page 133) and lemon wedges, if desired. Serves 4.

# Pan-Fried Fish



**This is so delicious and just takes ten minutes to prepare. The pan juices are great served with rice, and a side dish of dark greens completes a simple, healthy meal. Flounder has a mild, sweet taste and delicate texture that is easy like. You can also try sole or striped bass.**

1 large egg
2 tablespoons whole milk
½ cup bread crumbs (or cornmeal)
Kosher salt and freshly ground black pepper
2 to 3 tablespoons salted butter or olive oil
Four 6-ounce white flounder fillets, cut into strips or left whole
½ cup freshly squeezed lemon juice
½ cup white wine (optional)
¼ cup capers (optional)
¼ cup finely chopped flat-leaf parsley

1 In a bowl, whisk together the egg and milk. In a separate bowl, mix together the bread crumbs and season with salt and pepper to taste.

2 Heat butter or oil in a large heavy skillet over medium-high heat. Dip the fillets into the egg mixture then press into the bread crumbs to coat each side thoroughly. Place the fillets in the pan and cook for 3 to 4 minutes on each side until golden brown.

3 Add the lemon juice, and capers and wine, if using, to the pan and cook for another minute or two. Sprinkle the fillets with the parsley. Serve immediately.

**Serves 4**

## Variation

**Broil it:** You can broil the fish in the oven instead of frying. In this case, liberally butter a shallow baking dish and place the breaded fish in it, sprinkle with half the lemon juice and broil, on the middle rack, for about 3 minutes, until golden brown. Turn the fillets, sprinkle with the remaining lemon juice and top with ½ cup grated Parmesan cheese. Broil for another 2 to 3 minutes. Serve with finely chopped parsley. Serves 4.

Note: See page 214 regarding environment-friendly fish with low mercury levels.

# Steamed Whole Fish





**This is a traditional Chinese way of preparing fresh whole fish—gently steamed with just a little flavor added to let the sweet, delicate taste of the fish shine. If you are lucky enough to get fresh whole fish, don't do anything more to it than this simple preparation. The sizzling oil topping at the end melds everything together and makes for a great presentation.**

1 or 2 whole fish, 1½ to 2½ pounds total, such as striped bass, black sea bass, or rainbow trout (or substitute fish fillets) (see Note)
4 slices peeled fresh ginger, sliced into matchsticks
3 tablespoons peanut or canola oil
4 scallions, sliced into matchsticks
3 tablespoons low-sodium soy sauce

1 Clean and scale the fish. If the flesh is thick, make 3 diagonal slices across the thickest part of the body on each side of the fish.

2 Place the fish on a heatproof dish or platter that will fit inside a steamer or on a rack that will fit inside a wok. Spread the ginger matchsticks over the fish.

3 Bring a few inches of water to a boil in the steamer or wok. Place the dish in the steamer or wok. Cover and steam over high heat for 8 to 10 minutes for small fish or fillets, 10 to 12 minutes for a 1½-pound fish, or 16 to 18 minutes for a 2½-pound fish. Try not to uncover the steamer or wok while steaming.

4 While the fish is steaming, heat the oil in a small saucepan until smoking. Remove the dish with the fish from the steamer or wok. Tip the dish slightly to drain off some of the cooking liquid. Sprinkle the fish with the sliced scallions and the soy sauce. Carefully drizzle the hot oil over the fish—the oil will sizzle and splatter a bit. Serve immediately, family style, with chopsticks, or divide the fish into individual serving portions and spoon some scallions and sauce over the top.

**Serves 2 to 4**

**Tip** You'll get a sense of how long a fish will take to steam after making this dish once. The flesh should just flake when prodded with a fork and come off the bone without sticking. Overcooking will toughen the fish. Err on the side of undercooking, check and cover for a minute or two more, if needed.

Note: See page 214 regarding environment-friendly fish with low mercury levels.

# Shrimp Curry





**This is adapted from a cookbook Alice recently worked on and tested. She had never made curry before, but this slightly spicy, creamy, and rich stew has now become a family favorite. A restrained scoop of this curry over steamed rice, and some dark greens make for a great meal. Leftover curry can be reheated and tossed with cooked noodles the next day.**

2 tablespoons canola oil
1 tablespoon peeled and chopped fresh ginger
1 tablespoon chopped garlic
1 cup medium-dice carrot
½ cup medium-dice celery
½ cup medium-dice onion
Kosher salt
⅓ fish sauce
⅓ low-sodium soy sauce
3 tablespoons rice vinegar
Three 14-ounce cans light coconut milk
1 cup chicken broth
1 to 2 tablespoons Thai green curry paste
1 to 2 teaspoons Madras curry powder (optional)
1 cup medium-dice peeled potato
1 pound shrimp, peeled and deveined
1 bunch cilantro, coarsely chopped
¼ cup peanuts, toasted and crushed

1 In a large pan over medium heat, heat the oil, add the ginger and garlic, and cook for 2 minutes. Add the carrot, celery, onion, and salt, and cook for 10 minutes, or until the onions are translucent, stirring occasionally.

2 Add the fish sauce, soy sauce, and rice vinegar and reduce over medium-high heat, about 5 minutes. Stir in the coconut milk, broth, curry paste, and curry powder. Bring just to a boil, lower the heat, and simmer about 20 minutes. Add the potatoes, and continue to simmer until the potatoes are tender, about 30 more minutes. Taste and adjust the seasonings, if needed.

3 Add the shrimp and simmer until they are pink and cooked through, about 5 minutes. Ladle the curry into individual bowls and garnish with the cilantro and peanuts. Serve with lime wedges and steamed rice.

**Serves 4 to 6**

# Country-style Ribs



**This slow-cooker recipe simmers for hours and fills your house with a mouthwatering aroma. Its flavors are more subtle than meat simmered in bottled barbecue sauce, but sometimes it is nice to have something simple.**

4 pounds country-style pork ribs
1 onion, chopped
1 green bell pepper, cored, seeded, and chopped
2 celery stalks, chopped
2 cups beef broth
1 cup red wine
One 28-ounce can diced tomatoes
One 8-ounce can tomato sauce
Kosher salt and freshly ground black pepper

Add all of the ingredients to a slow cooker and cook on low for 7 to 8 hours until the meat starts to fall off the bones.

**Serves 6 to 8**

**Variation** Just add the meat and onion to the slow cooker along with an 18-ounce bottle of your favorite barbecue sauce and cook as instructed above.

**Leftovers** Use the leftovers to make a pasta sauce. Pull the meat off the bones and simmer the meat and left-over sauce with a little more tomato sauce, if needed.

# Pork Tenderloin with Shiitake Mushrooms



**Pork tenderloins are available at warehouse clubs and are great to keep on hand in the freezer. They are simple and quick to cook and are a good alternative to the ubiquitous chicken breast. This recipe makes two meals. Serve as an elegant dinner on the first night with greens, and freeze a tenderloin for another night.**

4 tablespoons honey
2 garlic cloves, chopped
2 tablespoons low-sodium soy sauce
2 tablespoons olive oil
Kosher salt and freshly ground black pepper
2 pork tenderloins, about 3 pounds
2 tablespoons vegetable oil
2 tablespoons favorite hot sauce
½ cup mayonnaise
½ Spanish onion, sliced
8 ounces shiitake mushrooms, sliced

1. Combine the honey, garlic, soy sauce, olive oil, and salt and pepper, and spread over the pork. Cover and refrigerate overnight for best results.
2. Preheat the oven to 400°F. Heat a large cast-iron skillet over medium-high heat and add the oil. When the oil is hot, add the pork and sear on all sides until brown. Transfer to the oven and cook for 10 to 15 minutes, until just done or the internal temperature reads 155°F on an instant-read thermometer. Remove the pork and set it aside to rest. Leave the cooking juices in the skillet.
3. While the pork is in the oven, mix the hot sauce with the mayonnaise in a small bowl and set aside.

4 To the skillet with the pork juices (remove some of the juices if you prefer a lighter sauce), add the onion and sauté on medium-high heat until soft, about 3 minutes. Add the mushrooms, reduce the heat to medium, and sauté until the vegetables are caramelized, 5 to 8 minutes.

5 Slice 1 tenderloin on the diagonal into ½-inch-thick pieces and serve with the mushrooms and spicy sauce on the side. Shred and freeze the second tenderloin for another meal.

**Serves 4**

## Variations

**Pork Tacos:** Shred the meat from the second tenderloin and reheat in a skillet with a little bit of water or broth. Serve with corn tortillas, chopped lettuce, cilantro, guacamole, and lime wedges. Serves 4.

**Slow Cooker Tenderloins:** Pork tenderloins are also easily prepared in the slow cooker. Just add 2 tenderloins and 16 to 18 ounces of your favorite barbecue sauce, and cook on low for 4 to 5 hours, until tender. Shred and freeze one tenderloin to serve over rice or in sandwiches for another meal.

# Slow Cooker Pork with Noodles



**This is a convenient meal-in-a-bowl recipe. In the morning before you leave home, just put the tenderloin in the slow cooker along with ingredients usually on hand, and pick up the fresh veggies on the way home to add to the cooker. It is a no-fuss meal with minimal cleanup for a weeknight!**

1 pork tenderloin, about 1½ pounds
6 cups chicken broth
¼ cup low-sodium soy sauce
¼ cup dry sherry (optional)
2 tablespoons dark brown sugar
4 garlic cloves, smashed
One 2-inch piece fresh ginger, peeled and sliced
2 pieces star anise (optional)
1 pound bok choy, roughly chopped
12 ounces dried rice vermicelli noodles
½ cup chopped fresh cilantro (optional)

1 For extra flavor, and if time permits, brown the tenderloin on all sides in an oiled cast-iron skillet over medium-high heat.

2 Put the pork, broth, soy sauce, sherry, sugar, garlic, ginger, and star anise, if using, into a 6-quart slow cooker. Cover and cook on high for 4 hours, or on low for about 8 hours.

3 During the last 20 minutes of cooking, add the bok choy to the slow cooker and cook on low.

4 Soak the rice noodles in hot water to cover about 10 minutes to soften, then add the noodles to the slow cooker for the last 5 minutes of the cooking. Make sure the noodles are submerged in the broth.

5 Remove the tenderloin from the cooker and shred the meat. Divide the noodles, meat, bok choy, and broth among four large soup bowls and sprinkle with cilantro. Serve immediately.

**Serves 4**

**Variation** Substitute pork shoulder, a fattier but tastier cut, and cook 8 hours on low. Spinach or frozen peas and basic spaghetti may be more familiar ingredients for pickier eaters. Add the spinach or peas during the last couple of minutes of cooking, then add the cooked spaghetti. For the adults, serve with Sriracha or favorite hot chili sauce on the side.

**Tip** Keep a tenderloin handy in the freezer and thaw overnight in the refrigerator. In the morning, put the meat into the slow cooker, you can skip the browning step, and proceed with Steps 2 through 5.

# Grilled to Perfection

**There's nothing like the mouthwatering sizzle of a backyard grill on a warm summer night. Start with a spicy rub or marinade, grill to perfection, and then finish off your dish with a delectable sauce.**

1 **Ready:** Apply marinade or rub of your choice (page 233).

2 **Set:** Start with a clean grill (see Step 5). Build a fire with charcoal stacked 2 or 3 deep. Once the briquettes have a red glow and are mostly covered in ash, 30 to 45 minutes, spread them out, leaving an area of the grill free of coals for indirect cooking. As with heating a skillet on the stovetop, if you can hold your hand 6 inches above the coals for only 2 seconds, it's at high heat; if 7 seconds, then it's at medium heat. Place the grate on the grill and allow to heat for a few minutes. (For slow cooking, rake the coals into 2 piles with a space between. An oven thermometer placed directly on the grate should read 325°F to 350°F.) Using paper towels and tongs, apply some cooking oil to the grate to prevent sticking.

3 **Grill:** Allow excess marinade to run off before placing the food on the grate over the coals. If food begins to char, move it to the charcoal-free area using tongs. Never use a fork on meat; piercing it will cause the juices to run out, and we don't want that! If there's a flare-up from marinade dripping on the fire, move it to the cooler portion of the grill temporarily or squelch the flame with the grill cover. (For slow cooking, place meat over a pan in the space between the coals to catch drips; you'll need to add about 10 briquettes per hour to each pile to maintain a temperature above 250°F.) Use the chart on pages 231 to 232 for approximate times for gas or charcoal grilling. For meat, firmness is an indication of doneness, or refer to the table on page 38.

4 **Sauce:** Serve grilled meats with your favorite jarred sauces or Pesto Sauce (page 252). Serve grilled poultry with Charmoula Sauce (page 252) or any of the dips on page 201. Serve grilled fish with Tartar Sauce (page 133) or Honey Dipping Sauce

(page 216). Serve grilled vegetables with any of the sauces on page 252 or the veggie dips on page 144. Other great accompaniments are Lemony Tahini Sauce (page 283), Tahini-Yogurt Dressing (page 147), Guacamole (page 146), Homemade Salsa (page 191), and Roasted Garlic (page 257).

5 **Cleanup:** After the grill has cooled a bit, use a wire grill brush to clean any stuck-on bits from the grate. Use tongs to wipe away residue with an oiled paper towel. Wait 24 hours before disposing of ash.



## Grill Chart

| INGREDIENT | | COOKING TIME |
|---|---|---|
| **Beef** | steaks, 1 inch | medium rare: 4 minutes per side on direct heat; 4 minutes on indirect heat |
| | hamburger patties | medium: 5 minutes per side on direct heat |
| **Sausages** | links | 10 minutes on indirect heat; turn once |
| **Pork** | chops, ½ inch | 3 minutes per side on direct heat |
| | kebabs | 15 minutes on direct medium heat, turning every 2 to 3 minutes |
| **Chicken** | wings | 25 minutes on indirect heat, covered |
| | drumsticks, thighs, and breasts | 45 minutes on indirect heat, covered |

## Grill Chart (continued)

| | | |
|---|---|---|
| **Seafood** | shrimp | 1 to 2 minutes per side on direct heat, covered |
| | tuna steaks, 1 inch | 2 minutes per side on direct heat, covered |
| | salmon fillets | 4 to 5 minutes per side on direct heat, covered |
| **Vegetables** | onions, peppers, zucchini, eggplant | 5 minutes per side on direct heat, covered |
| | asparagus | 8 minutes on direct medium heat, turning once, covered |
| | corn (in husks) | 15 minutes on direct medium heat and 5 minutes on indirect heat, turning every 2 to 3 minutes, covered |
| | tomatoes | 15 minutes on direct heat in aluminum foil, turning once, covered |
| | potatoes | 30 minutes on direct heat in foil, turning once, covered |

## Marinades and Rubs

You can brush your meat, poultry, or seafood with some mustard or pesto sauce, smear on a paste of garlic, chopped herbs, olive oil and lemon juice, or simply season with lots of cracked black pepper and sprinkle with salt. If you have the time, though, try the following:



**Honey Mustard Marinade:** Combine ½ cup soy sauce, ⅓ cup olive oil, 4 teaspoons honey, 3 tablespoons Dijon mustard, 2 tablespoons chopped herbs, 2 tablespoons minced garlic, 1 teaspoon apple cider vinegar, kosher salt, and freshly ground black pepper. Put about 2 pounds of meat or poultry into a gallon-sized plastic bag and refrigerate for at least 1 hour, flipping the bag halfway through the marinating time so it marinates evenly. The bigger the cut of meat, the longer it should marinate. Remove it from the refrigerator and let it come to room temperature before cooking.

**Basic Rub:** In a bowl, combine ⅓ cup coarsely granulated salt, ¼ cup firmly packed light brown sugar, ¼ cup sweet paprika, 2 tablespoons dried thyme leaves, 2 tablespoons dried oregano, 2 tablespoons freshly ground or cracked black pepper, and 1 tablespoon cayenne. Make sure to break up the brown sugar. Transfer to an airtight container and store in a cool, dark place, or refrigerate for up to 6 months. Seasons 5 to 10 pounds of meat, poultry, or seafood. Seafood is best grilled within an hour of rubbing.

**Curry Rub:** For a flavorful but not-too-hot Indian influence, leave out the thyme and oregano in the Basic Rub and stir in 4 tablespoons of a blend of curry powder, turmeric, cardamom, and ground ginger, in proportions to your liking.

**French Rub:** Replace the oregano in the Basic Rub with France's "king of herbs," tarragon. Great for grilling or roasting chicken.

**Middle Eastern Rub:** Great for lamb. Cut the paprika in the Basic Rub in half and replace it with garlic powder. Use several sprigs of fresh thyme instead of dried, and substitute onion powder for the tablespoon of cayenne. Grill or roast with lots of olive oil.

# Beef Stew





**This is a simple recipe that requires very little in order to produce superior results—but the little things are crucial. The quality of the meat itself really does matter. The cut should be chuck, rump, or round, preferably from grass-fed beef. The pieces of meat should be cut into 1½- to 2-inch cubes—any smaller and you run the risk of overcooking the meat and drying it out. Lastly, the temperature must be kept very low. We prefer to cook stews in the oven in a covered enameled Dutch oven because the heat is more easily controlled. A temperature of 250°F to 300°F is perfect for a long, slow braise. This stew reheats and freezes well. It will keep refrigerated for 3 to 4 days.**

3 tablespoons flour, preferably Wondra
3 pounds stewing beef, preferably chuck, rump, or the round, cut into 2-inch cubes
3 tablespoons olive oil or other vegetable oil
1 large Spanish onion or 3 medium yellow onions, peeled and coarsely chopped
1 celery stalk, diced
1 garlic clove, peeled and flattened
1 bay leaf
1 sprig thyme or ½ teaspoon fresh thyme leaves
3 cups beef stock, red or white wine, or a combination
6 carrots, peeled and cut into 2-inch lengths
3 medium potatoes, peeled and cut into large cubes

1 Preheat the oven to 300°F. Put some of the flour on a plate. Dry the pieces of beef with paper towels, then roll them in the flour to coat lightly.

2 Heat 2 tablespoons of the oil in a heavy Dutch oven. Sauté the meat in batches until it is browned on all sides. Do not crowd the pan; if you do, the meat will steam instead of brown. When the meat is browned, remove from the pot and set it aside.

3 Add the remaining tablespoon of oil to the pot. Add the onion and celery and sauté until soft, about 7 minutes. Add the garlic, bay left, thyme, and stock to the pot.

4 Return the meat to the Dutch oven, cover, and place it in the oven. Check the stew after 30 minutes. The liquid should be simmering gently. If it isn't, adjust the heat. Cook for 1 hour, then add the carrots and potatoes. Continue to cook until the meat is fork-tender, about 1 hour more. Serve the stew warm over rice or egg noodles, or with crusty bread.

**Serves 6**

## Variations

- Add a few tablespoons of chopped fresh tomato or a tablespoon of tomato paste.
- Add green beans, sautéed mushrooms, or peas during the last 30 minutes of cooking.
- Add a teaspoon of chopped fresh rosemary, a strip of orange zest, and some black olives for a Mediterranean flavor.
- On a busy day, make the stew in your slow cooker. Prepare the meat, onion, and celery according to Steps 1 through 3 and place them in a large slow cooker. Add the carrots. Slow cook on high for 4 to 5 hours, or on low for 7 to 8 hours. Serve the stew with mashed potatoes.

# Turkey Shepherd's Pie

**Ground turkey is a healthy substitute for ground beef in a lot of recipes, and kids won't notice the difference. Yogurt in the mashed potato topping is also a lot healthier than the traditional butter and cream, and if you want to avoid dairy altogether, you can even mash the potatoes with just a few tablespoons of olive oil. The ingredients make enough turkey-veggie mixture to freeze for another meal. Add a little marinara sauce when reheating the mixture and serve it over pasta. Or use it to make the Turkey Chili in the Variation.**

**Topping**

3 pounds small red potatoes
1 cup plain fat-free or low-fat Greek-style yogurt
Kosher salt and freshly ground black pepper

**Filling**

1 tablespoon plus 1 teaspoon extra-virgin olive oil
1 large onion, chopped
3 celery stalks, chopped
1 pound frozen or fresh mixed, diced vegetables (such as corn, carrots, green beans)
2 garlic cloves, minced
3 pounds lean ground turkey
2 teaspoons kosher salt
1 tablespoon chopped fresh thyme
1 teaspoon chipotle or regular chili powder
Freshly ground black pepper
2 tablespoons plus 1½ teaspoons cornstarch
1½ cups frozen peas
6 ounces tomato paste
⅓ cup ketchup

1 Preheat the oven to 425°F. Make the topping: Place the potatoes in a saucepan and cover with cold water by 2 inches. Bring to a boil, reduce the heat to low, and cook until fork-tender, about 20 minutes. Drain the potatoes and reserve 2 cups of the cooking liquid. Mash the potatoes with a potato masher. Stir in the yogurt. Season with salt and pepper to taste and set aside.

2 Make the filling: Heat the oil in a medium cast-iron skillet over medium heat. Add the onion, celery, frozen vegetables, and garlic, and cook, stirring, until tender, about 10 minutes.

3 Add the ground turkey and cook, breaking up any large pieces, for 5 minutes. At this point, remove about half (roughly 5 cups) of the turkey-veggie combo and reserve for chili (recipe follows).

4 Stir the salt, thyme, and chili powder into the remaining mixture. Season with freshly ground black pepper. Whisk together the cornstarch and reserved cooking liquid and add to the turkey mixture. Boil for 1 minute, until the mixture thickens. Stir in the peas. Add the tomato paste and ketchup and mix well.

5 Transfer the filling to a 2-quart round or oval baking dish and top with the mashed potatoes. Bake the pie until bubbling and the top is browned, about 35 minutes.

**Serves 6 to 8**

## Variation

**Turkey Chili:** Heat the 5 cups reserved turkey-veggie mixture from the recipe above in a large pot over low heat. Add six 15-ounce cans kidney beans, rinsed and drained, one 25.5-ounce jar tomato sauce, 5 teaspoons chili powder, 4 teaspoons paprika, and 2 teaspoons ground cumin. Cook over low heat for 20 minutes. Season with salt and pepper to taste and adjust the other spices as desired. If you like your chili hotter, you can add red pepper flakes or cayenne pepper as well, to taste. Serve the chili piping hot over rice. Serves 6 to 8.

# Turkey-Spinach Meat Loaf





**This is a delicious way to get spinach into your little ones without much protest—they will gobble it up! This recipe makes two loaves. Divide and freeze the second loaf in portions to use in the different ideas for leftovers suggested on the following page.**

2 pounds lean ground turkey
2 onions, chopped and sautéed
One 10-ounce bag fresh spinach, chopped fine (about 6 cups)
1 bunch flat-leaf parsley, finely chopped
1 cup bread crumbs
3 tablespoons Dijon mustard
2 large egg whites
2 teaspoons kosher salt
1 teaspoon freshly ground black pepper
½ cup ketchup

1 Preheat the oven to 400°F. In a large bowl, combine the turkey, onions, spinach, parsley, bread crumbs, mustard, egg whites, salt, and pepper.

2 Divide the mixture in half and place each half in a 9 x 5 x 3-inch loaf pan or shape into free-form loaves on a baking sheet. Spread the top of each meat loaf with the ketchup.

3 Bake until cooked through, approximately 50 minutes.

**Makes 2 loaves; each loaf serves 5 to 6**

## Leftover Ideas

**Stuffed Pasta Shells:** Cook one 16-ounce box of jumbo pasta shells according to the package directions. Drain and set aside. Preheat the oven to 375°F. Lightly oil a 13 x 9-inch baking dish. In a large saucepan, sauté 1 chopped onion and 2 minced garlic cloves in a tablespoon of olive oil for about 5 minutes over medium-high heat. Add 2 cups crumbled leftover meat loaf and 1 cup jarred pasta sauce and bring to a simmer. Add ½ cup of the tomato sauce to the prepared dish. Stuff the pasta shells with the meat-loaf mixture, place into baking dish, and top with another ½ cup tomato sauce, 1 cup shredded mozzarella cheese, and ½ cup shredded Parmesan cheese. Bake for 45 minutes. Serves 6.

**Serve with spaghetti:** Heat 2 cups of crumbled meat loaf with tomato sauce and serve over spaghetti. Add a little water to thin out the sauce, if necessary.

**Serve with mashed potatoes:** Melt 2 tablespoons butter over medium-high heat and saute 2 cups of crumbled meat loaf for about 5 minutes. Add 2 tablespoons flour and cook for 3 minutes. Add 1 cup chicken broth and a dash of Worcestershire sauce and simmer for 10 minutes. Serve over mashed potatoes. Serves 4.

**For pizza or sandwiches:** Crumble the meat loaf and use as a pizza topping, or slice the meat loaf for cold or grilled sandwiches.

# Thin Linguine with Turkey Meatballs

**Every once in a while, Alice's husband will make a large batch of these meatballs on a weekend afternoon. The extra meatballs are frozen for future low-hassle dinners. Individual meatballs with a bit of sauce can be stored in the refrigerator or freezer for little ones' lunches and snacks.**

**Sauce**

3 tablespoons olive oil
4 garlic cloves, minced
5 cups canned, crushed tomatoes
½ teaspoon dried oregano
¼ teaspoon dried thyme
Kosher salt and freshly ground black pepper

**Meatballs**

1 large egg
⅓ cup whole milk
1¼ teaspoons kosher salt
¼ teaspoon freshly ground black pepper
1 white onion, finely chopped
½ cup porcini mushrooms, finely chopped
⅔ cup plain bread crumbs
1 cup freshly grated Parmesan cheese
½ cup chopped flat-leaf parsley
1 pound ground turkey (light and dark meat)
1 pound thin linguine

1 Make the sauce: In a large frying pan, heat the oil over medium-high heat. Add the garlic and cook about 1 minute. Stir in the tomatoes, oregano, and thyme, and season to taste with salt and pepper. Bring to a boil, lower the heat, and simmer, covered, for 25 minutes.

2 Make the meatballs: In a large bowl, whisk together the egg, milk, salt, and pepper. Stir in the onion, mushrooms, bread crumbs, ¼ cup of the grated cheese, and the

chopped parsley. Add the ground turkey and mix gently but thoroughly. With slightly wet hands, to keep the meatballs from sticking, form the mixture into 1¼-inch balls and place them on a sheet of wax paper.

3 Using a wooden spoon, transfer the meatballs to the frying pan with the sauce and spoon the sauce over to coat. Cook the meatballs over medium-low to medium heat until they are just cooked through, about 10 minutes.

4 In a large pot of boiling salted water, cook the linguine according to the package instructions until al dente. Drain and serve with the meatballs, sauce, and the remaining ¾ cup grated cheese.

**Serves 4**

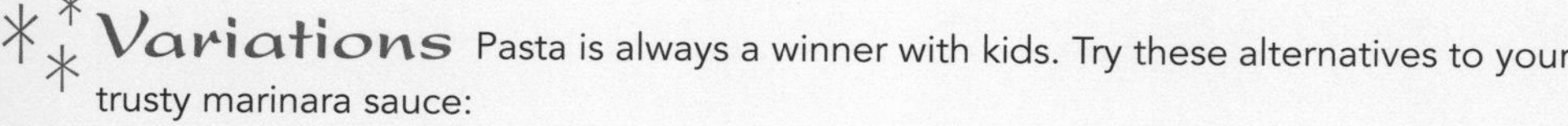

**Variations** Pasta is always a winner with kids. Try these alternatives to your trusty marinara sauce:

- Add chopped clams sautéed in butter, garlic, and parsley.
- Add veggies stir-fried with olive oil, garlic, and herbs.
- Add flaked tuna, peas, a splash of cream, and Parmesan cheese.
- Add snap peas, soy sauce, fresh ginger, chopped peanuts, toasted sesame seeds, and sesame oil.
- Add pesto with peas or chopped green veggies like broccoli, asparagus, or green beans.
- Instead of making meatballs, just sauté the ground meat and onions, then add the other ingredients minus the egg and milk to make a hearty meat sauce to serve over pasta.

**Tip** Alice's middle daughter has a sensitivity to gluten so her family has switched to wheat-free pastas. While some brands of rice pastas are passable substitutes, we actually love the taste and texture of quinoa spaghetti. Quinoa's great nutritional profile is an added bonus.

# Vegetable Lasagna

**Alice could not decide whether to include this recipe in the book or not. It's a family favorite but it is a time commitment to put together in the morning when she would rather stay in bed! The recipe is handed down from her mother-in-law, adapted from an old magazine published more than twenty years ago, and her children demand it a few times a year. What is so great about it is all the vegetables and just the right explosion of flavors without being over-the-top rich. It is a lasagna you can feel good about serving and eating. Take an hour one morning to make it and enjoy your evening with only a salad to toss together while the lasagna bakes in the oven.**

**Sauce**

2 teaspoons olive oil
¾ cup minced onion
1½ cups sliced mushrooms
2 garlic cloves, minced
Two 14½-ounce cans tomatoes, chopped, with their juices
¼ cup minced flat-leaf parsley
¼ cup dry red wine
One 6-ounce can tomato paste
2 teaspoons dried basil
1½ teaspoons dried oregano
1 teaspoon dark brown sugar
Kosher salt and freshly ground black pepper

**Lasagna**

Two 10-ounce packages frozen chopped spinach, thawed and drained
One 12-ounce carton low-fat cottage cheese
1 large egg, beaten
10 dry lasagna noodles, whole wheat or brown rice
5 cups thinly sliced zucchini, about 1¼ pounds
1¼ cups (5 ounces) finely shredded part-skim mozzarella cheese
2 tablespoons Parmesan cheese

1. Make the sauce: Heat the oil in a large pot over medium-high heat. Add the onion and sauté for 3 minutes. Add the mushrooms and garlic and sauté for 2 minutes. Add the remaining sauce ingredients and stir well. Reduce the heat and simmer, uncovered, for 20 minutes. Remove from the heat and set aside.
2. Press the spinach between paper towels to get rid of excess moisture. In a medium bowl, combine the spinach, cottage cheese, and egg, and stir well. Set aside.
3. Assemble the lasagna: Lightly oil a 15 x 10 x 2-inch baking dish. Spoon one-third of the sauce into the dish. Arrange 4 to 5 noodles in a single layer over the sauce. Top with half of the spinach mixture, patting and spreading it over the noodles with the back of a fork. Layer half of the zucchini over the spinach and sprinkle with ½ cup of the shredded mozzarella cheese. Repeat the layering (sauce, noodles, spinach, zucchini, mozzarella) and top with the last third of the sauce. Cover and refrigerate the lasagna for 8 hours to soften the noodles and meld the flavors.
4. Preheat the oven to 350°F. Bake the lasagna, covered, for 1½ hours. Uncover and sprinkle with the remaining ¼ cup mozzarella cheese and the Parmesan cheese. Let stand 5 minutes before cutting and serving.

**Serves 6 to 8**

## Variation

**Cheater's Lasagna:** Preheat the oven to 400°F. In a large pot over a medium flame, heat 1 tablespoon olive oil. Add 1 diced onion and cook 5 minutes. Add 1 pound crumbled sausage meat and cook until no longer pink, about 10 minutes. Add one 26-ounce jar marinara sauce and heat for 3 minutes. Add 1 pound cooked ziti and toss. Add ½ cup grated Parmesan cheese, one 15-ounce container ricotta cheese, and one 10-ounce package frozen spinach, thawed and squeezed, and toss again. Spread the mixture in a 13 x 9-inch baking dish and sprinkle with 1 cup shredded part-skim mozzarella. Bake for about 15 minutes, until the mozzarella melts. Let cool 5 minutes before serving. Serves 4.

# Veggies & Sides

# Buying Organic

## PRODUCE

**There is no better reason to buy organic produce than to reduce the amount of pesticide residue that enters our bodies. Not to mention the delicious flavor of fruits and vegetables grown by farmers with love for the earth. These "best-to-worst" lists rank vegetables and fruits by the number of pesticides found, with the greatest number at the bottom, so buy organic versions of these first.**

Source: Environmental Working Group and foodnews.org

## VEGGIES (BEST TO WORST)

**onions** (least number of pesticides)
**corn**
**avocados**
**asparagus**
**sweet peas**
**eggplant**
**cabbage**
**sweet potatoes**
**mushrooms**
**kale/collard greens**
**lettuce**
**potatoes**
**sweet bell peppers**
**spinach**
**celery**

---

## FRUITS (BEST TO WORST)

**pineapple** (least number of pesticides)
**mangoes**
**kiwi**
**cantaloupe** (domestic) (low in pesticides, but scrub thoroughly and eat soon after slicing to avoid bacterial contamination)
**watermelon**
**grapefruit**
**honeydew melon**
**plums** (domestic)
**cranberries**
**bananas**
**cantaloupe** (imported) (low in pesticides, but scrub thoroughly and eat soon after slicing to avoid bacterial contamination)
**grapes** (domestic)
**oranges**
**red raspberries**
**plums** (imported)
**pears**
**blueberries** (domestic)
**apples**
**strawberries**
**peaches**

# Steamed Vegetables with Sauces

**Steaming is a gentle way to cook your vegetables and a cooking method that retains more of their pure flavor and nutrients. The simplest additions to steamed veggies are a little melted butter, a squeeze of lemon juice, a splash of extra-virgin olive oil, balsamic vinegar, or soy sauce, or a sprinkle of chopped herbs, Parmesan cheese, or toasted sesame seeds. If you are feeling a little bored and a little energetic, try the sauces on page 252 for added zing.**

1. In a large pot, bring about 2 inches of water to a boil over medium-high heat and place a steamer basket or folding metal basket on top.
2. Add the vegetables, cover, and steam according the recommended time below. If you are steaming for a long period, check that the water has not boiled away.
3. If you are not serving the vegetables warm and want crisp vegetables, have a bowl of cold water ready to shock the steamed vegetables to stop the cooking.

**Artichokes:** 20 to 45 minutes, until outer leaves can be easily pulled off

**Asparagus:** thin spears, 3 to 4 minutes; thick spears, 5 to 6 minutes

**Beets:** 30 to 35 minutes

**Broccoli:** florets, 4 to 5 minutes; spears, 5 to 6 minutes

**Brussels sprouts:** 7 to 11 minutes

**Cabbage:** wedges, 6 minutes

**Carrots:** ¼-inch slices, 6 to 8 minutes

**Cauliflower:** head, 12 to 15 minutes; florets, 4 to 6 minutes

**Green beans:** 4 to 5 minutes

**Kale:** 4 to 5 minutes

**Spinach:** 4 to 5 minutes

**Sweet potatoes:** whole, 40 to 50 minutes; 1-inch pieces, 15 minutes

**Winter squash:** peeled, 2-inch pieces, 15 to 20 minutes

**Zucchini:** ¼-inch slices, 5 to 7 minutes

## Sauces

**Toasted Garlic and Coriander Oil:** In a small saucepan, cook 2 tablespoons olive oil with 2 tablespoons minced garlic for about 3 minutes over medium-low heat. Stir in 2 teaspoons ground coriander and cook for 20 seconds. Squeeze a wedge of lemon over 1 pound steamed vegetables and toss with the oil.

**Balsamic-Bacon Vinaigrette:** In a small saucepan over medium heat, cook 2 slices bacon until crisp and golden, about 5 minutes. Transfer to paper towels to drain, then dice or crumble into small pieces. Add 1 small minced shallot to the bacon fat left in the pan and cook, stirring, for about 1 minute. Add 1½ tablespoons balsamic vinegar and scrape the pan to loosen the browned bits. Remove from the heat and add 1 tablespoon lemon juice and ¼ teaspoon Dijon mustard. Whisk in 3 tablespoons olive oil. Toss the dressing with 1 pound steamed vegetables and sprinkle with the bacon bits.

**Pesto Sauce:** This is a versatile sauce to accompany vegetables and meats or to use in pizzas, pastas, or sandwiches. In the bowl of a food processor fitted with the steel blade, combine ½ cup toasted pine nuts, 4 cups fresh basil or flat-leaf parsley leaves, ½ cup grated Parmesan cheese, 1 minced garlic clove, and kosher salt and freshly ground black pepper. With the machine running, slowly add ½ cup extra-virgin olive oil. Process until smooth. Toss ½ to 1 cup pesto with 1 pound steamed vegetables. The pesto will keep, covered, in the refrigerator for 2 to 3 days. Or divide and freeze it in ice-cube trays to have available whenever you need it. Makes about 2 cups.

**Charmoula Sauce:** This is a Moroccan pesto than can also be served with fish and poultry. In a food processor, coarsely chop ½ cup fresh cilantro, ½ cup fresh flat-leaf parsley, and 5 garlic cloves. Add ⅓ cup lemon juice, 2 teaspoons sweet paprika, 2 teaspoons kosher salt, 1½ teaspoons ground cumin, and ½ cup olive oil, and pulse until the sauce has the consistency of a rough pesto. Toss ½ to 1 cup sauce with 1 pound steamed vegetables. The sauce can be made 2 days in advance, covered, and refrigerated. Bring to room temperature 1 hour before serving. Makes about 1 cup.

# Winter Vegetable Medley

**Every Christmas, guests go to Natasha's house and say one thing or another about Brussels sprouts—"I really never eat them" or "I really don't like them." They change their minds in a big hurry after tasting these. The key is not to overcook them in the first place, and not to overcook them in the second place. In any case, they are great by themselves or with other vegetables.**

- Approximately ¾ pound Brussels sprouts, trimmed and halved
- 1 pound baby carrots
- 12 small potatoes (such as fingerlings or new potatoes), halved or quartered
- 6 small zucchini, cut into chunks
- 3 tablespoons olive oil, plus more for the baking sheet
- 4 onions, 1 finely diced, 3 quartered
- 6 garlic cloves, peeled and minced
- 1 cup walnuts, whole or chopped
- Kosher salt and freshly ground black pepper

1 Preheat the oven to broil. Lightly oil a baking sheet.

2 Steam the Brussels sprouts, carrots, potatoes, and zucchini until just barely tender, about 5 minutes. Rinse under cold running water, drain, and set aside.

3 Heat the olive oil in a large, deep frying pan. Add the diced onions and sauté for about 5 minutes over medium heat, until soft and translucent but not browned.

4 Add the garlic and sauté for 2 minutes. Turn off the heat and add the vegetables and walnuts to the onion and garlic in the frying pan. Season to taste with salt and pepper. Turn the contents of the pan out onto the prepared baking sheet and spread the vegetables out in a single layer.

5 Put the vegetables in the oven. Let broil for 2 minutes, then shake the pan and broil for 2 minutes more, or until the veggies are browned and crispy on top. Watch carefully to avoid burning. Serve warm or at room temperature.

**Serves 8**

# Basic Roasted Vegetables

**We're not sure if there is anything more satisfying than a pan of nutritious, colorful vegetables roasting in the oven while you prepare the rest of the meal. Following is a guide to roasting times; roast for longer if you like your vegetables more tender to add to pasta, pizza, or salads.**

1 to 2 pounds vegetables, peeled, trimmed, and cut into to 1-inch pieces
1 to 3 tablespoons extra-virgin olive oil
Kosher salt and freshly ground black pepper
1 lemon
1 teaspoon low-sodium soy sauce (optional)

1 Preheat the oven to 400°F. Line a heavy-duty, rimmed baking sheet with parchment paper.

2 In a large bowl, toss the vegetables with 1 to 2 tablespoons olive oil. Season to taste with salt and pepper. Arrange the vegetables on the prepared baking sheet in a single layer. Roast until tender (see roasting times opposite). If you are roasting a variety of vegetables, it is best to roast them on separate baking sheets, or to add them at intervals, to allow for the different roasting times, and then combine them at the end of the roasting.

3 Drizzle the roasted vegetables with more extra-virgin olive oil and a squeeze of lemon, or 2 teaspoons lemon juice and 1 teaspoon soy sauce. Or try any of the sauces on page 252.

**Serves 4 to 8**

**Asparagus:** 5 to 8 minutes on one side, 5 to 8 minutes on the other

**Beets:** 15 minutes on one side, 10 to 15 minutes on the other

**Broccoli:** 10 minutes, stir, and roast another 5 minutes

**Brussels sprouts:** halved and roasted cut side down about 15 minutes

**Butternut squash:** 15 minutes on one side, 5 to 10 minutes on the other

**Carrots:** 10 to 15 minutes on one side, 5 minutes on the other

**Cauliflower:** 20 to 30 minutes, stirring every 10 minutes

**Green beans:** about 15 minutes

**Mushrooms:** 20 minutes on one side, 5 to 10 minutes on the other

**Potatoes:** 10 to 15 minutes on one side, 5 minutes on the other

**Sweet potatoes:** 10 minutes on one side, 5 to 10 minutes on the other

**Zucchini:** 10 to 15 minutes on one side, 5 minutes on the other

## Variation

**Roasted Garlic:** This is a fantastic accompaniment to practically any roasted meat, serve it with just a great loaf of crusty bread, or add it to mashed potatoes or pasta salads. Preheat the oven to 350°F. Slice off the tops of some garlic heads to expose the cloves. Drizzle each head with 1 tablespoon extra-virgin olive oil and season with salt and pepper. Wrap each head in aluminum foil and roast 20 to 30 minutes, until soft. Serve whole or scoop or squeeze the garlic pulp from its papery skin.

# Eat Your Colors!

**Remember to get as much color variety in your family's diet as possible. The colors of fruits and vegetables are a small clue to their range of nutrients. By eating a variety of different-colored fruits and vegetables, you are guaranteed a diverse assortment of essential vitamins and minerals.**

## GREEN

artichokes, arugula, asparagus, avocados, broccoli, broccoli rabe, brussel sprouts, celery, chayote squash, chinese cabbage, cucumbers, endive, green apples, green beans, green cabbage, green grapes, green onion, green pears, green peppers, honeydew, kiwifruit, leafy greens, leeks, lettuce, limes, okra, peas, snow peas, spinach, sugar snap peas, watercress, zucchini

## WHITE

bananas, brown pears, cauliflower, garlic, ginger, jerusalem artichoke, jicama, kohlrabi, mushrooms, onions, parsnips, potatoes, shallots, turnips, white corn, white nectarines, white peaches

## RED

beets, blood oranges, cherries, cranberries, guava, papaya, pink grapefruit, pink/red grapefruit, pomegranates, radicchio, radishes, raspberries, red apples, red bell peppers, red chili peppers, red grapes, red onions, red pears, red peppers, red potatoes, rhubarb, strawberries, tomatoes, watermelon

## YELLOW/ORANGE

apricots, butternut squash. cantaloupe, cape gooseberries, carrots, golden kiwifruit, grapefruit, lemon, mangoes, nectarines, oranges, papayas, peaches, persimmons, pineapples, pumpkin, rutabagas, sweet corn, sweet potatoes, tangerines, yellow apples, yellow beets, yellow figs, yellow pears, yellow peppers, yellow potatoes, yellow summer squash, yellow tomatoes, yellow watermelon, yellow winter squash

## BLUE/PURPLE

black currants, black salsify, blackberries, blueberries, eggplant, elderberries, grapes, plums, pomegranates, prunes, purple Belgian endive, purple potatoes, purple asparagus, purple cabbage, purple carrots, purple figs, purple grapes, purple peppers, raisins

# Asparagus with Mustard Vinaigrette

**Here is a perfect recipe for the arrival of the first spring asparagus. Early-season asparagus only requires a gentle steaming and a light dressing. We prefer to use the rice vinegar as it is milder than the balsamic for the little ones.**

1½ pounds asparagus, well washed, tough ends snapped off
½ cup extra-virgin olive oil
¼ cup rice vinegar or 3 tablespoons balsamic vinegar
3 tablespoons Dijon mustard
1 garlic clove, minced
½ bunch flat-leaf parsley or cilantro leaves, minced

1 Steam the asparagus until tender, about 4 minutes for thin spears or about 8 minutes for thick spears. For thick spears, you can use a vegetable peeler to peel off the tough outer skin from the middle to the thick end of each spear before steaming. Transfer the asparagus to a large bowl of ice water to stop the cooking. Drain, wrap in paper towels, and set aside or refrigerate until ready to serve.

2 In a bowl, whisk together the oil, vinegar, and mustard until well blended. Whisk in the minced garlic and parsley or cilantro.

3 Arrange the asparagus on a plate and drizzle the dressing over the top. Serve cold or at room temperature.

**Serves 4**

## Variation

**Asparagus and Veggie Toss:** Cut the asparagus into 1½-inch pieces and follow Steps 1 and 2 in the preceding recipe. In a mixing bowl, toss the steamed asparagus with 1 peeled and sliced cucumber or 1 red bell pepper, cut into 1½-inch strips. Toss with half of the mustard vinaigrette and minced parsley. Taste and add more vinaigrette, if desired. Serves 4 to 6.

## Alternatives

**Roasted Asparagus with Parmesan:** Preheat the oven to 450°F. Wash and trim 1½ pounds asparagus. On a rimmed baking sheet, toss the asparagus with 2 tablespoons olive oil and season with salt and pepper. Spread out in an even layer and sprinkle with ¼ cup finely grated Parmesan cheese. Roast for 10 to 15 minutes until tender. Serves 4.

**Roasted Asparagus with Sesame Seeds:** Preheat the oven to 450°F. Wash and trim 1½ pounds asparagus and cut into 2-inch lengths. On a rimmed baking sheet, toss the asparagus with 2 tablespoons olive oil and season with salt. Spread out in an even layer and roast for about 10 minutes. Then toss the asparagus, sprinkle with 1½ teaspoons sesame seeds, and continue roasting until tender, about 5 minutes more. Serves 4.

**Roasted Asparagus Tart:** See page 175.

**Stir-fried Asparagus with Shiitake Mushrooms:** Substitute 1 pound asparagus, tough ends snapped off and sliced into 1-inch pieces, for the sugar snaps in Stir-fried Sugar Snaps with Shiitake Mushrooms (page 301).

# Avocado, Corn, and Black Bean Salsa

**Buy a couple of avocados weekly. This excellent, highly nutritious fruit is an easy addition to meals. Simply slice it and serve with a mustard vinaigrette (page 260) or dice it and add it to salads or smoothies. This simple salsa recipe is for inspiration; the elements can be changed: eliminate what is not available or what you don't like and add diced red peppers, edamame, red onion, cilantro . . . whatever you prefer.**

- 2 tablespoons extra-virgin olive oil
- 1 cup corn kernels
- 1 jalapeño pepper, seeded, membranes removed, finely chopped (optional)
- 2 tablespoons peeled and minced fresh ginger
- 1 cup diced tomatoes
- 2 firm, ripe avocados
- ½ cup canned black beans, rinsed and drained
- ¼ cup freshly squeezed lime juice
- Kosher salt and freshly ground black pepper

1. Heat the oil in a medium frying pan over medium heat. Add the corn kernels, jalapeño, if using, and ginger and cook 2 minutes, stirring. Add the tomatoes and cook 2 minutes, stirring, until the corn and tomatoes are softened. Let cool slightly.
2. Halve the avocado lengthwise, remove the pit, peel, and dice (see Tip).
3. In a bowl, toss the avocado, black beans, corn-and-tomato mixture, and lime juice to combine. Season to taste with salt and black pepper. Serve immediately over mixed greens or as an accompaniment to grilled chicken or pork.

**Serves 4**

## Alternatives

**Avocado and Egg Toss:** Hard-boil 2 eggs per person and cut the whites into bite-size pieces; reserve the egg yolks for another use, like crumbling over a salad. Toss with diced avocado, a drizzle of olive oil, and salt and pepper.

**Make a Dressing:** See Power Dressing (page 307).

**Make a Dip:** See Guacamole (page 146) and Guaca-Salsa (Tip, page 307).

**Tip** Keep unripe avocados at room temperature or store in a brown paper bag with a banana to speed up the ripening. Once ripe, you can store avocados in the refrigerator for several days. To pit an avocado, run a chef's knife around the avocado lengthwise and twist the halves in opposite directions to separate. Carefully chop down on the pit with the knife blade to attach it, then use the knife to twist the pit out of the avocado. Use a pairing knife to cut into the flesh and use a spoon to scoop out the flesh. Serve immediately after cutting as avocado discolors quickly.

# Beans, Beans, Beans

Remember this school yard song? "Beans, beans, they're good for your heart. The more you eat, the more you %&$!" Beans *are* good for your heart. Half the world's population thrives on the bean-and-grain combo instead of meat (see Good to Know on the following page). Each 1-cup serving of adzuki beans, for example, is packed with 17 grams of protein and contains no heart-damaging fat. Beans are a great source of complex carbohydrates—which are better for kids than simple sugars—as well as iron, magnesium, and potassium.

Dried beans are more economical, lower in sodium, and tastier than canned. They also contain more vitamins and minerals. Cook up a batch and divide into 1- or 2-cup portions to put into the freezer. Add them to soups and salads, purée them into tomato sauces for pasta, or serve them with rice. Use the following chart as a guide to different types of beans and their soaking and cooking times. Cooking dried beans in the slow cooker is convenient—you don't have to worry about something simmering on the stove. In general, a pound of dried beans (2 to 2½ cups) yields about seven 1-cup servings.

1. Soak 1½ to 2 pounds dried beans. See chart on page 266 for recommended soaking times in plenty of cool water.
2. Drain and rinse the beans. Pick over and discard bad beans.
3. Add the beans to a large stockpot or 6-quart slow cooker. Cover with water plus 2 inches, leaving several inches of clearance to the top of the stockpot or slow cooker. For stovetop cooking, bring the water to a boil, lower the heat, and simmer until the beans are tender (see chart for estimated cooking time). For slow cooking, cover and cook until the beans are tender (see chart for estimated cooking time).
4. Toward the end of cooking, add up to 2 teaspoons salt per pound of beans (adding salt too early counteracts the softening effect of the water, creating a tougher skin).
5. Let cool. Store the beans with the cooking liquid in airtight containers or plastic storage bags. The beans will keep in the refrigerator for up to 4 days and in the freezer for up to 6 months.

**Makes 10 to 15 cups**

**Good to Know** Eaten alone, beans are an incomplete protein, which means that they lack some of the nine essential amino acids, and should be consumed in combination with complementary rice, barley, or another grain. Practically every culture has a favorite combination: rice and beans, hummus and pita bread, chili and corn-bread, refried beans with tortillas, lentils and rice. It is best for growing bodies to get the completed protein combination at once, rather than consuming it separately throughout the day.

## Bean Soaking and Cooking Times

| TYPE | SOAKING TIME | STOVETOP | SLOW COOKER |
|---|---|---|---|
| Adzuki | none | 1 hour | 5–8 hours on low |
| Black | 6 hours–overnight | 45–60 minutes | 1½–2 hours on high |
| Black-eyed peas | 6 hours–overnight | 1 hour | 1½–2 hours on high |
| Chickpeas | overnight | 1–1½ hours | 4–5 hours on low |
| Fava, already peeled | none | 1–2 hours | 5–8 hours on low |
| Kidney, white (cannellini, Great Northern, marrow, navy) | 6 hours–overnight | 1–1½ hours | 2–3½ hours on high |
| Kidney, red | overnight | 1–1½ hours | 5–8 hours on low |
| Lentils, red | none | 20–30 minutes | 5–8 hours on low |
| Lentils, green | none | 30–45 minutes | 5–8 hours on low |
| Lima | overnight | 60–90 minutes | 4–5 hours on high |
| Lima, baby | overnight | 45–50 minutes | 2–3½ hours on high |
| Mung | overnight | 1–1½ hours | 8 hours on low |
| Split peas | none | 35–40 minutes | 4–5 hours on high |
| Pinto | overnight | 1½ hours | 2–3½ hours on high |
| Soybeans, tan or yellow | overnight | 3–4 hours | 6–8 hours on high |
| Soybeans, black or brown | overnight | 1–1½ hours | 2–3½ hours on high |

# Breaded Sautéed Broccoli

**Steamed broccoli "trees" are popular enough with little ones. And a dusting of Parmesan cheese can make them even more appealing. But for a slight twist, try breading the broccoli before sautéing—kids will love the extra crunch.**

1 to 1½ pounds broccoli
2 large eggs, lightly beaten
1 cup fine bread crumbs, preferably whole wheat
¼ cup olive oil
Kosher salt and freshly ground black pepper

1. Peel off the tough skins on the stems and cut the broccoli into bite-size florets and pieces. Steam the broccoli just until tender, about 5 minutes, and transfer to a bowl of ice water to stop the cooking.
2. Drain the broccoli and pat dry with paper towels. Dip the pieces into the beaten egg, transfer to a large bowl, and toss with the bread crumbs.
3. Heat the oil in a large cast-iron skillet over medium heat. When the oil is hot, add the broccoli. Sauté until browned and tender, about 5 minutes. Season with salt and pepper to taste. Serve immediately.

**Serves 4**

## Variations

- Garnish with chopped flat-leaf parsley and a squeeze of fresh lemon juice.
- Add ¼ cup each chopped almonds and golden raisins halfway through the cooking, in Step 3.
- Add ¼ cup grated Parmesan cheese to the bread crumbs before tossing with the broccoli, in Step 2.

## Alternatives

**Broccoli and Cauliflower Salad:** Exercise those little molars with this powerful raw duo. (It will be easier for kids if you cut the florets into small, less than 1-inch, pieces.) Mix 2 cups each broccoli and cauliflower florets with ¼ cup each mayonnaise and vegetable oil, 2 tablespoons apple cider vinegar, and salt and pepper to taste. Refrigerate for a few hours. Mix in a few tablespoons crumbled bacon, raisins, and sunflower seeds just before serving. Serves 4 to 6.

**Stir-fried Broccoli:** Prepare the broccoli as in Step 1. Follow the instructions for Stir-fried Sugar Snaps with Shiitake Mushrooms (page 301). Increase the stir-frying time slightly, and add a little more water. Cook until the broccoli is heated through. Serves 4.

# Butternut Squash
## with Lemon, Walnuts, and Parsley

**Butternut squash is loaded with fiber and vitamins A and C. It even comes in pre-peeled, diced, and ready-to-cook packages at some supermarkets, so there is no excuse not to make this a regular part of your family's diet. Steam it, roast it, sauté it, and add it to salads or use it in soups (page 107).**

- 2 tablespoons extra-virgin olive oil
- 2 tablespoons unsalted butter
- 3 cups ½-inch dice, peeled butternut squash, about 2 pounds
- Kosher salt and freshly ground black pepper
- ¼ cup chopped flat-leaf parsley
- ½ cup chopped walnuts, toasted
- 1½ teaspoons freshly grated lemon zest

1. Heat the oil and butter in a large cast-iron skillet over medium-high heat. Add the squash, season with salt and pepper to taste, and cook, stirring occasionally, until tender, 8 to 10 minutes.
2. Put the cooked squash, parsley, walnuts, and lemon zest into a serving bowl and toss to combine. Serve immediately.

**Serves 4**

## Variations

- Toss together the squash, oil, salt, pepper, and walnuts on a rimmed baking sheet and roast at 400°F for 20 to 30 minutes. Toss with the lemon zest and parsley just before serving.

- Substitute diced sweet potatoes for the squash. Follow Step 1, then add ½ cup water and cook over medium heat, stirring, until the water has evaporated and the potatoes are tender and browned, about 10 minutes more. Continue with Step 2.

- Sauté 2 cups butternut squash as in Step 1 and add 1 pound sautéed or steamed fresh spinach halfway through the cooking.

## Alternative

**Butternut Squash Purée:** Slice 1 butternut squash in half lengthwise. Scrape out the seeds and stringy center with a spoon. Place both halves, face down, in a roasting pan and add 1 inch of water. Bake in a 350°F oven until tender, about 45 minutes. Scoop out the flesh of the squash and add to a bowl. Cut in 4 tablespoons (½ stick) unsalted butter and 2 tablespoons maple syrup and mash with a potato masher. Season to taste with salt. Purée in a food processor. Serves 4.

# Sautéed Cabbage





**Cabbage is one of the most nutritious vegetables, rich in antioxidants and vitamins. While white or green cabbages are more popular, be sure to add red cabbage, which contains even more nutrients, to your diet. It has a robust flavor and when sautéed turns a bright purple, which may impress little ones.**

- 1 tablespoon olive oil
- 1 tablespoon unsalted butter
- 1 cup thinly sliced or chopped purple onion
- 3 cups thinly sliced red cabbage
- Kosher salt and freshly ground black pepper

Heat the oil and butter in a large pan over medium-high heat. Add the onion and cook until tender, about 5 minutes. Add the cabbage, salt, and pepper, and sauté until softened and cooked through, about 5 minutes.

**Serves 4**

## Alternatives

**Quick Cabbage Slaw:** Whisk together ¼ cup each freshly squeezed lemon juice and olive oil. Season to taste with salt and pepper and toss with 4 cups shredded napa or red cabbage, 4 thinly sliced scallions, and ¼ cup chopped fresh cilantro. Serves 4.

**Cabbage with Spaghetti and Bread Crumbs:** For finicky eaters, try pairing cabbage with spaghetti. Melt 1 tablespoon unsalted butter in a sauté pan with 1 minced garlic clove and cook for about 1 minute. Stir in ½ cup bread crumbs and cook, stirring, about 5 minutes until golden, and set aside. In a separate pot, melt 2 tablespoons unsalted butter and add 4 to 5 cups shredded savoy or green cabbage. Season with salt and pepper and cook, stirring, until wilted, 3 to 4 minutes. Add ½ cup water and cook, covered, for another 4 minutes. Uncover and stir in 3 tablespoons cream. Cook until the sauce has thickened, about 2 minutes. Add 8 ounces cooked spaghetti with ½ cup pasta cooking water and stir to combine. Cook for 1 minute, then add ¼ cup grated Parmesan cheese. Sprinkle with the reserved bread-crumb mixture and serve immediately. Serves 4.

# Simple Caesar Salad

**This is probably many a child's introductory salad—what's not to like about the creamy sauce paired with mild crunchy greens, Parmesan cheese, and croutons?**

**Dressing**
¼ cup fresh lemon juice
¼ cup light mayonnaise
¼ cup grated Parmesan cheese
2 anchovy fillets, roughly chopped (optional)
1 small garlic clove

1 large head romaine lettuce, torn into pieces
¼ small red onion, finely sliced
½ cucumber, peeled and finely sliced
1 cup croutons

1. In a blender, combine all of the ingredients for the dressing and blend until smooth.
2. In a salad bowl, toss the lettuce, onion, and cucumber with ½ cup or more of the dressing, as desired. Sprinkle with the croutons and serve immediately.

**Serves 4**

## Variations

- Add protein: Top the salad with grilled or broiled chicken breast, leftover Broiled Salmon (page 216), shrimp, or scallops, or add 2 quartered, hard-boiled eggs.
- Add shavings of carrot and Parmesan cheese.
- Try the dressing with a salad of steamed baby potatoes, green beans, and roasted red peppers.

# Carrot and Jicama Salad

**Carrots are easy—always have some baby carrots and hummus in your fridge for a quick snack or an addition to the dinner table. For a bit of variety, though, here is a refreshing and easy new favorite. Jicama is a root vegetable that is a good source of fiber and vitamin C. It has a mild sweet flavor with a crisp texture and is good raw—serve it with carrot and celery sticks. Cooked—use it in recipes calling for water chestnuts.**

1 large carrot, peeled and cut into julienne
1 small jicama, peeled and cut into julienne, or substitute green apple or celery
½ bunch cilantro, roughly chopped
2 to 3 limes
1 tablespoon sesame oil
Pinch of kosher salt

In a medium bowl, mix together the carrots, jicama, and cilantro; it is best if you have an equal amount of carrot and jicama. In a small bowl, mix the juice from 2 of the limes with the oil. Season with salt, taste, and add more lime juice, if desired. Toss the vegetables with the dressing and serve immediately.

**Serves 4**

## Variations

- Try shaving the carrot and jicama into long ribbons with a sharp vegetable peeler instead of cutting them into julienne. Toss in a few tablespoons of walnuts or pecans.
- Try a different dressing: Mix 2 tablespoons each olive oil and apple cider vinegar with a tablespoon of honey.

## Alternative

**Glazed Carrots:** Don't forget this simple classic. Put 1 pound carrots, cut into coins or sticks, 2 tablespoons unsalted butter, ⅓ cup water or stock, and salt and freshly ground pepper to taste into a saucepan. If you like your carrots sweeter, add 1 tablespoon sugar or maple syrup. Bring to a boil and simmer until the carrots are tender and the liquid has evaporated, 10 to 20 minutes. Garnish with a bit of chopped flat-leaf parsley, or a sprinkle of chopped walnuts or pecans, or raisins or dried currants. Serves 4.

# Cauliflower and Apple Purée

**Cauliflower purée is an elegant vegetable side and, when mellowed with a little milk and apple, it is delectable for the entire family. Serve this with any roasted meat or poultry in place of mashed potatoes.**

2 pounds cauliflower, cored and coarsely chopped
1 small apple, peeled, cored, and chopped
1 quart low-fat or whole milk
Kosher salt
1 to 2 tablespoons unsalted butter
1 tablespoon heavy cream (optional)

1 Put the cauliflower, apple, milk, and ½ teaspoon salt in a large saucepan and bring to a gentle boil over medium heat. Cover and cook, stirring halfway through the cooking time, until the cauliflower is tender, 20 to 25 minutes.

2 Drain the cauliflower and apple and reserve the cooking liquid. Transfer the solids to a food processor and purée until perfectly smooth, adding a little of the cooking liquid, if necessary. Add the butter, the cream, if using, and salt to taste. The reserved cooking liquid can also be used in the soup variation that follows.

**Serves 4 to 6**

## Variation

**Cauliflower Soup:** In a medium saucepan, using a combination of the reserved cooking liquid and chicken broth, whisk together equal amounts of liquid and cauliflower and apple purée. Bring to a simmer over medium heat and season to taste. Top with crispy crumbled bacon, if desired.

# Eggplant with Sesame Sauce





**Asian eggplants, both the Chinese and Japanese varieties, are about 1½ to 2 inches in diameter and 5 or 6 inches long. They have thinner skins, fewer seeds, and a more delicate, sweet flavor. Both countries have favorite ways of serving them. A typical Japanese method is to quickly fry the eggplant and serve it with a light sauce—simple and delicious.**

8 Asian eggplants, about 2 pounds
Canola oil for frying
¼ cup chicken broth
¼ cup low-sodium soy sauce
½ teaspoon peeled and grated fresh ginger
1 tablespoon sesame seeds, toasted

1 Trim off the ends of eggplants. Make 4 incisions lengthwise down each eggplant, about one third of the way deep into the flesh, within ½ inch of the ends, and spaced ⅛ inch apart.

2 Heat about ¾ inch oil in a wok or a large, wide frying pan just until smoking. Carefully fry the eggplants, in batches, for about 4 minutes, turning occasionally. The eggplants should be soft when pressed. Transfer the eggplants to paper towels to drain excess oil and let cool. Cut the eggplants on the diagonal into 1½-inch pieces. Refrigerate, if desired.

3 Whisk together the broth, soy sauce, and ginger and pour over the eggplants. Sprinkle with the toasted sesame seeds. Serve chilled or at room temperature.

**Serves 4 to 6**

## Alternatives

**Stir-fried Eggplant with Pork:** A little pork goes a long way when paired with "meaty" eggplant. Slice 1½ pounds Asian eggplants diagonally into 1-inch pieces. Heat 3 tablespoons peanut oil in a wok or large frying pan over medium-high heat. Add 2 minced garlic cloves and ¼ pound ground pork and stir-fry until the pork is no longer pink, about 2 minutes. Add the eggplants and stir-fry for 2 minutes. Add 1 cup chicken broth, cover, and cook for 8 minutes, until the eggplants are tender. Stir in 2 to 3 tablespoons oyster sauce. To thicken the sauce, add 1 tablespoon cornstarch mixed with 2 tablespoons water. Cook for 1 or more minutes until the sauce thickens and the eggplants are as tender as you like. This is scrumptious served over rice. Serves 4 to 6.

**Baba Ganoush:** See page 147.

# Green Beans with Cilantro

**Haricots verts, or French green beans, are best in this recipe, if you can find them. Kids love these skinny, green "fries." They cook in less time than regular green beans and remain crunchy without tasting raw. This is a favorite in Alice's family.**

1 pound haricots verts or green beans, trimmed
4 teaspoons apple cider vinegar
2 tablespoons extra-virgin olive oil
1 shallot, minced
½ cup minced cilantro
2 tablespoons sesame seeds, toasted (optional)

1. In a large pot of boiling water, blanch the haricots verts for 3 to 5 minutes until tender; fresh haricots verts will cook fast; some vacuum-packaged beans will take longer. When the beans are cooked but still crisp, drain and transfer to a large bowl of ice water to stop the cooking. Drain again and set aside, or wrap in paper towels and refrigerate until ready to serve.
2. Whisk together the vinegar and oil in a serving bowl. Add the minced shallot and cilantro. Toss the beans with the dressing and sprinkle with the toasted sesame seeds, if using.

**Serves 4**

## Variations

**Two Bean Salad:** Trim and cut 1 pound haricots verts in half or into 1-inch pieces. Prepare as instructed in Step 1. In a medium bowl, whisk together 2 tablespoons each Dijon mustard, red wine vinegar, and extra-virgin olive oil. Add the reserved beans and one 15-ounce can rinsed and drained cannellini beans and mix well. Season to taste with salt and pepper. Serves 4 to 6.

**Haricots Verts with Lemony Tahini Sauce:** Prepare the haricots verts as instructed in Step 1. Whisk together 1 minced and mashed garlic clove, 3 tablespoons tahini paste, and 3 tablespoons lemon juice. Add water, a teaspoon or so at a time, until you reach a creamy consistency. Drizzle the tahini sauce over the haricots verts. Serves 4.

# Great Greens Sauté

**"Eat your vegetables" is an old refrain to kids, but these days it's evolved into an even more challenging: "Eat your dark green leafy vegetables!" Dark green leafy vegetables—which include spinach, kale, chard, and collards—are an excellent source of fiber and provide many essential vitamins and minerals your body needs. They are rich in calcium, iron, vitamins A and C, and supply vitamins E, K, and B6, thiamin, folate, riboflavin, magnesium, manganese, and potassium. Each type of green has a slightly different nutrient profile—for example, our bodies can absorb more calcium from kale than spinach—so try to rotate different greens into your menu. The recommended serving size per person of cooked greens is ½ cup—aim to serve them at least two to three times a week.**

- 1 pound dark greens, such as kale or Swiss chard, well washed
- 2 tablespoons olive oil
- 1 shallot, thinly sliced
- 1 garlic clove, crushed
- 1 tablespoon unsalted butter
- ¼ cup grated Parmesan cheese
- ¼ cup toasted pine nuts or walnut pieces
- Kosher salt and freshly ground black pepper

1. Remove the thick stems from the chard, if using, and slice thinly. Roughly chop the kale or chard leaves into 2-inch pieces.
2. Heat the oil in a large, heavy-bottomed pot over medium-high heat. Add the shallots and garlic and cook until soft, about 5 minutes. Add the stems and sauté about 4 minutes. Add the leaves and cook, tossing well, about 5 minutes more, or until wilted and tender.
3. Transfer the greens to a serving bowl, add the butter, and toss until melted. Mix in the cheese and pine nuts and season with salt and pepper to taste.

**Serves 4**

**Variation** Instead of the cheese and pine nuts, mix in 2 tablespoons apple cider vinegar or balsamic vinegar.

## Ideas

- Slowly cook kale in a little bit of chicken broth and stir it into pasta or risotto, or serve as a side to braised meats.
- Cut kale leaves into ¾-inch-wide strips and serve raw as a salad with grated Parmesan, toasted nuts, and a lemon juice and olive oil vinaigrette.
- Boil Swiss chard, drain, and add to cheesy egg dishes for breakfast.
- Sauté Swiss chard in a little olive oil and garlic and use it to top pizzas or crostini.
- See also Baked Kale Chips (page 148), Fried Farro with Collard Greens (page 308), and Red Peppers with Quinoa Stuffing (page 294).

# Chinese Greens with Oyster Sauce

**This recipe is a standard in Chinese home cooking. There is usually stir-fried meat and vegetables going, a fish steaming, and a pot of water boiling, ready for the leafy greens—all timed and coordinated so everything is ready and served hot at the same time. It is a handy recipe for busy cooks to know.**

1½ pounds bok choy, Chinese broccoli, or Asian greens (or substitute broccoli rabe or broccolini)

2 tablespoons peanut oil

3 tablespoons oyster sauce

1. Cut the greens into 2-inch pieces, separating the leaves from the stems. If using baby bok choy, just cut them in half lengthwise.
2. Add enough water to a large pot to cover the vegetables by 2 inches. Lightly salt the water, add the oil, and bring to a boil.
3. Add the vegetable stems and cook for 3 minutes; add the leaves and let the water return to a boil. Check for tenderness and cook 1 or 2 minutes more, if desired.
4. Transfer the vegetables to a serving plate or bowl with a bit of the cooking liquid for moisture. Top with the oyster sauce and serve immediately.

**Serves 4**

## Variations

For a lighter touch, replace the oyster sauce with ¼ cup cooking liquid and 2 tablespoons soy sauce.

**Seared Baby Bok Choy:** Follow Steps 1 through 3 until the bok choy halves are just tender. Place the bok choy, cut side down, on paper towels to drain. Heat 2 tablespoons oil in a large, wide, cast-iron skillet over medium-high heat. Add the bok choy in batches, cut side down, and let cook until slightly charred. Top with Balsamic-Bacon Vinaigrette (page 252).

# Mashed Peas

**Peas are probably the vegetable most successfully frozen and most kids love them, so always have them in your freezer. Cooked just until tender, served plain or with a sprinkle of grated cheese, or tossed into pastas or risottos, they are a quick and easy vegetable any night. If you want to fuss with them occasionally, try them mashed and serve them as a bed for fish, or mix some into mashed potatoes.**

One 10-ounce package frozen peas
½ cup chicken stock, milk, or heavy cream
1 tablespoon unsalted butter
Kosher salt and freshly ground black pepper

1. Bring a shallow pot of lightly salted water to a boil over medium-high heat. Add the frozen peas and cook for 3 to 5 minutes until tender.
2. In a small saucepan, heat the chicken stock, milk, or heavy cream.
3. Drain the peas and transfer to a blender or food processor. Add half the liquid, the butter, and salt and pepper to taste and blend. Add more liquid, if desired, and process to the desired consistency. The peas are good coarsely or smoothly puréed. If you like them really coarse, you can use a potato masher. Taste and adjust the seasonings, and serve immediately.

**Serves 2 to 4**

## Variations

**Herbed Peas:** Add ¼ cup fresh mint leaves, some fresh basil, and tarragon to the preceding recipe and purée.

**Add a vegetable:** Add steamed cauliflower or a few boiled potatoes to the purée for a heartier dish.

## Alternatives

**Peas and Cheese Frittata:** Make Kitchen Sink Frittatas (page 66) with 1½ cups peas and ½ cup grated cheese of your choice.

**Mini Ham and Pea Quiches:** See page 172.

**Peas and Asparagus:** Peas and diced carrots are a familiar duo, but for a more elegant combination try peas with asparagus. Cook 1 minced shallot in 3 tablespoons unsalted butter in a cast-iron skillet over medium heat until tender, about 3 minutes. Add 1 to 2 cups asparagus, cut into 1-inch pieces, and cook about 2 minutes, stirring. Add one 10-ounce package thawed frozen peas, cover, and cook for about 5 minutes until tender. Add ¼ cup chopped fresh basil and salt to taste. Serves 4 to 6.

# Smashed Red-skinned Potatoes



**This is an easier, lower-fat version of the classic mashed potatoes. The potatoes don't need to be peeled, and there's no need for dairy. The red—or Red Bliss—potatoes have a naturally creamy texture that is enhanced by the olive oil. And you can throw in whatever seasonings you like: roasted garlic, flavored oils, or chopped herbs.**

- 2 pounds small red potatoes, preferably Red Bliss
- 3 to 4 tablespoons extra-virgin olive oil
- 2 tablespoons chopped flat-leaf parsley
- Kosher salt and freshly ground black pepper

1. Put the potatoes in a large pot and cover with cold water by 2 inches. Bring to a boil, reduce the heat, and simmer until the potatoes are slightly overcooked, about 20 minutes; their skins will crack and the potatoes will split easily when pierced with a fork.
2. Drain the potatoes and add 3 tablespoons olive oil to the pot. Mash with a potato masher. Add the chopped parsley and salt and pepper to taste. For a creamier texture, add a little more oil.

**Serves 4 to 6**

## Variations

- Add a clove or two of peeled garlic to the potatoes as they are boiling. The garlic will become soft and can be mashed along with the potatoes. Alternatively, scoop out the garlic from a head of roasted garlic (page 257), and add to Step 2.
- Substitute 2 tablespoons chopped fresh chives for the parsley and add a couple of spoonfuls of low-fat Greek-style yogurt for a smoother texture and a tangy flavor.

**Good to Know** Potatoes have gotten a bad reputation because they are usually fried to death and because of their association with the dreaded white carbs. In fact, they are a good source of fiber and vitamins. Colored potato varieties have the additional healthy benefit of carotenoids and flavonoids. When not drowned in butter or sour cream, potatoes are actually a low-calorie vegetable. Moms should feel good about serving small baked potatoes topped with a bit of cheese and broccoli florets; just make sure the kids eat the skins for the extra fiber.

# Red Peppers with Quinoa Stuffing

**Not only are red peppers great raw, stir-fried, roasted, and grilled, but they can also be a great vessel to stuff with all sorts of goodies. A bit of ground beef, rice, and tomato sauce is a classic combination. Here is an updated version made with quinoa and kale. Use this recipe as a starting point and decide what your kids will be comfortable with—sausage instead of quinoa would probably be greeted with more enthusiasm!**

1 cup chicken or vegetable stock
½ cup quinoa
3 large red bell peppers
2 tablespoons extra-virgin olive oil
1 medium onion, chopped
2 garlic cloves, minced
¾ pound kale leaves, lightly steamed, squeezed dry, and chopped
¼ cup grated Parmesan cheese
¼ cup toasted pine nuts
1 tablespoon freshly squeezed lemon juice
Kosher salt and freshly ground black pepper

1. Preheat the oven to 400°F. In a medium pot, bring the stock to a boil. Add the quinoa, cover, and simmer for 15 minutes.
2. Meanwhile, halve the peppers lengthwise through the stems, leaving them attached. Remove the seeds and trim the large membranes. Lightly brush the peppers with 1 tablespoon of the oil. Place, cut side down, in a baking dish. Bake until the peppers are just tender, 10 to 15 minutes. Let cool slightly.

3 Heat the remaining 1 tablespoon oil in a large cast-iron skillet over medium heat. Add the onion and cook, stirring, until softened, about 5 minutes. Add the garlic and kale and cook 2 minutes. Remove the skillet from the heat and let cool slightly. Stir in the cooked quinoa, Parmesan cheese, pine nuts, and lemon juice. Season to taste with salt and pepper.

4 Place the 6 pepper halves, cut side up, in a baking dish. Divide the filling among the pepper halves. (You can prepare and stuff the peppers in advance to this point and refrigerate them for up to 2 days.) Add a bit of water to the baking dish and cover with aluminum foil. Bake for 15 to 20 minutes; uncover and bake for 5 minutes more. Serve hot.

**Serves 6**

## Variations

**Quinoa with Kale:** Eliminate the red peppers and double the stock, quinoa, and kale in the preceding recipe. Proceed with Steps 1 and 3 only. Serve warm or at room temperature as a side dish. Serves 4 to 6.

**Stuffed Portobello Mushrooms:** Use 6 medium portobello mushroom caps instead of the red peppers and reduce the final baking time to 10 to 15 minutes, until heated through. Or try stuffing the mushroom caps with 1½ cups cooked spinach mixed with 1 cup ricotta cheese. Top each stuffed mushroom with 1 to 2 tablespoons marinara sauce. Serves 6.

# Baked Spinach Gratin

**Spinach is an excellent source of vitamins but most moms can't convince kids to eat enough of it. Creamed spinach is a favorite dish, but somehow serving equal amounts of heavy cream and spinach feels like you are canceling out any health benefits. Try this baked spinach gratin with a little bit of stock and cheese. Leftovers can be made into a spinach omelet in the morning—your kids will be thrilled.**

3 tablespoons (½ stick) unsalted butter
3 pounds fresh spinach, stemmed and well washed, or three 10-ounce packages frozen chopped spinach, thawed
1½ tablespoons flour
1 cup beef or chicken stock
Kosher salt and freshly ground black pepper
½ cup grated Parmesan cheese
¼ cup grated Gruyère cheese
3 tablespoons fine bread crumbs

1. Preheat the oven to 375°F. Lightly butter a 1-quart baking dish with 1 tablespoon of the butter.
2. If using fresh spinach, steam it in a steamer over boiling water for 3 minutes until tender. (You can also boil the spinach quickly, but you loose more of the nutrients.) Drain the spinach, squeeze out the excess liquid, and chop roughly. If using frozen, thawed, spinach, squeeze out as much liquid as possible.

3 Melt the remaining 3 tablespoons butter in a large frying pan over medium heat. Cook the spinach for 2 to 3 minutes, until any remaining liquid has evaporated. Reduce the heat, sprinkle with the flour, and stir for about 2 minutes to cook the flour. Stir in the stock, simmer a few minutes, and season with salt and pepper to taste.

4 Stir the Parmesan cheese into the spinach and transfer the mixture to the prepared baking dish. Mix the Gruyère cheese with the bread crumbs and sprinkle on top of the spinach. Bake until heated through and slightly brown on top, about 30 minutes.

**Serves 6**

## Alternative

**Japanese-style Spinach:** Sometimes just serving a vegetable at a different temperature or in a different form makes it new and appealing. Prepare 1 pound fresh spinach as in Step 2. Sprinkle with a little salt and 1 tablespoon soy sauce. Shape the drained, squeezed spinach into a 1-inch-thick log and slice crosswise into 1-inch rounds. Dip a flat side of each round into toasted sesame seeds and arrange on a plate, sesame side up. Drizzle with a bit of sesame oil and more soy sauce, if desired. Serves 2 to 4.

# Sugar Snaps with Orange-Honey Dressing

**When the farmers' market has sugar snaps, we cannot wait to make this recipe. We buy extra as they tend to disappear during the prep phase—it is hard to resist just eating the sugar snaps raw. Alice likes to quickly blanch the sugar snaps in boiling water, but you can certainly skip this step, if you like.**

1 pound sugar snaps or snow peas, stems removed
2 tablespoons freshly squeezed orange juice
2 tablespoons rice or wine vinegar
1 teaspoon honey
½ teaspoon low-sodium soy sauce
2 tablespoons peanut oil
1 teaspoon sesame oil
2 scallions, sliced on the diagonal (optional)
½ teaspoon peeled, grated fresh ginger (optional)
2 teaspoons sesame seeds, toasted (optional)

1 In a pot of boiling water, blanch the sugar snaps for 30 seconds to 1 minute until crisp-tender; they should still be very crisp. Immediately plunge them into a bowl of ice water to stop the cooking. Drain, wrap in paper towels, and refrigerate until ready to serve.

2 In a serving bowl, whisk together the juice, vinegar, honey, soy sauce, oils, and the scallions and ginger, if using. Toss the cooked sugar snaps with the dressing in the bowl and sprinkle with the sesame seeds, if using.

**Serves 4**

## Alternatives

**Sugar Snap, Radish, and Cucumber Salad:** Prepare the sugar snaps as in Step 1. Add 1 peeled and sliced large cucumber and 8 to 10 trimmed and thinly sliced radishes. Toss with 1 tablespoon seasoned rice vinegar and 1 teaspoon apple-cider vinegar. Sprinkle with ¼ cup toasted sesame seeds, if desired. Serves 4 to 6.

**Stir-fried Sugar Snaps with Shiitake Mushrooms:** This cooking method works well later in the season, when sugar snaps are tougher, or you can substitute snow peas. Heat 1 tablespoon canola oil in a wok or large frying pan over medium-high heat. Add 1 cup thinly sliced shiitake mushrooms and 1 tablespoon low-sodium soy sauce and stir-fry for a few minutes to soften. Add 1 teaspoon canola oil and 1 pound trimmed sugar snaps and quickly stir-fry for another 30 seconds. Add 1 tablespoon soy sauce and a splash of water and stir-fry until the peas are crisp-tender and the liquid has reduced to a glaze. Serve immediately. Serves 4.

# Sweet Potato Fries



**Sweet potatoes are one of the best vegetables you can eat. They are loaded with carotenoids, vitamin C, potassium, and fiber. Bake these sweet potato fries and serve them regularly. And experiment with using a mixture of sweet and regular potatoes in some of your favorite recipes (see Tip).**

1½ pounds sweet potatoes, peeled or unpeeled and scrubbed, cut into ¼-inch-square sticks
1 tablespoon grated Parmesan cheese (optional)
1 tablespoon olive or other vegetable oil
¼ teaspoon garlic powder
¼ teaspoon paprika
¼ teaspoon kosher salt
¼ teaspoon freshly ground black pepper

1 Preheat the oven to 450°F.

2 Combine all of the ingredients in a large bowl. Mix thoroughly, then transfer to a baking sheet lined with parchment paper. Spread out the potatoes in a single layer.

3 Bake until the potatoes are tender and golden brown, turning occasionally, 20 to 30 minutes. Let cool slightly before serving.

**Serves 4**

**Tip** Use sweet potatoes: Sweet potatoes are less starchy than white potatoes so they don't substitute as well in all recipes where the potato's texture is important, such as with mashed or scalloped potatoes. Instead, try using 1 sweet potato to 3 whites of equal size for added nutritional value without giving up texture.

## Alternatives

**Baked Sweet Potatoes:** Preheat the oven to 400°F. Pierce the sweet potatoes several times with the tines of a fork and place on a rimmed baking sheet. Bake until tender, 45 to 60 minutes depending on their size. Make a slit in the top of each potato and add 1 tablespoon butter. Season with salt and pepper, paprika, or a mixture of cinnamon and brown sugar. Serve half a potato per person.

**Mashed Sweet Potatoes:** Scoop out the insides of baked sweet potatoes and mash together with a bit of butter and cream or olive oil. Season with salt and pepper to taste and serve hot.

**Sweet Potato Chips:** See page 149.

**Sautéed Sweet Potatoes:** Heat 2 tablespoons olive oil in a large nonstick frying pan over medium heat. Add 2 cups cubed sweet potato and cook, stirring, until it begins to soften, 8 to 10 minutes. Add ½ cup water or broth and ½ cup chopped red onion. Cook until the liquid has evaporated and the potatoes are tender and browned, about 10 minutes. Season with salt and pepper and a dash of balsamic vinegar, if desired.

# Preserving Nutrients

**Eat your veggies! You've heard it over and over since childhood: a healthy diet is one that is plant based. Even your grandmother knew this. But did you know that a fresh fruit or veggie is transported an average of 1,700 miles from its field to your supermarket? Produce loses nutrients in transit. Unless your produce is locally farmed, it might be better to choose frozen over fresh. Frozen food is flash frozen at the farm, after washing and other processes are finished, to retain maximum nutrient value. How you store and cook your produce also affects how much value is retained.**

## AIR EXPOSURE

This is where nutrient loss occurs through transit in fresh foods or the amount of time spent in the freezer before a food is eaten. Vitamin C is by far the most susceptible to destruction through air exposure. A fresh veggie can lose up to 75 percent of its vitamin C in a week. While frozen veggies retain more nutrients than canned or fresh over time, there is little nutrient value left in food that has been frozen for over a year.

## CANNING

Canning is a high-heat process that can destroy much of the vitamins and nutrients in fruits and vegetables. During the canning of tomato juice, up to 70 percent of the original folic acid can be lost. Yet canned beans are a suitable substitute for dried beans, as heating does not damage protein, fiber, and minerals in the same way as it can damage vitamins and other nutrients.

## COOKING

Boiling in large quantities of water is the greatest cause of nutrient loss, followed by cooking in small pieces. Short cooking times with little water cause the least damage. Roasting veggies also retains nutrients, as well as leaving veggies in large pieces.

## ADDED ELEMENTS

While it preserves color, baking soda saps nutrient content, so don't buy processed fruits and veggies with added baking soda or add it during cooking. Generally, no preservatives are added during flash freezing.

Nowadays, since most of us can't visit the farmers' market every day, grow our own, or find freshly picked veggies in our local stores, the foods we eat have less nutrients than they did a hundred years ago. Still, whether fresh, frozen, or canned, veggies and fruits are nutritious as well as good sources of fiber and phytochemicals, like beta-carotene and lycopene. So don't sweat too much over your choice of cooking and storage method, just eat your fruits and vegetables!

# Five-Star Salad Bar

**You probably have more on hand in your refrigerator than you think to throw together a tasty, leafy salad. So you and your children never have to have the same salad twice if you don't want to. Try mixing and matching five main ingredients for something a little different every time.**

**Base:** arugula, butter lettuce, endive, escarole, iceberg lettuce, mesclun salad, mixed greens, red cabbage, romaine lettuce, spinach.

**Fruit & Veggies:** apple slices, artichoke hearts, avocados, bean sprouts, carrots, corn kernels, grapes, tomatoes, green onions, jicama, mangoes, mushrooms, olives, pear slices, peppers, radishes, tangerine slices.

**Protein Goodies:** bacon, black beans, cheddar cheese cubes, chicken, chickpeas, cottage cheese, feta, goat cheese, hard-boiled eggs, Swiss cheese, tuna.

**Dressings:** bleu cheese, buttermilk, Caesar dressing (page 275), ranch, Dijon vinaigrette, Power Dressing (page 307), herbed oil and vinegar, lemon juice.

**On the Top:** cashews, croutons, fresh herbs, pine nuts, raisins, dried cranberries, sesame seeds, shaved Parmesan cheese, walnuts.

# Power Dressing

**Avocados are one of the few fruits that provide "good" fats and provide nearly twenty essential nutrients, including fiber, potassium, vitamin E, B-vitamins and folic acid. Cilantro contains many plant derived chemical compounds that are known to have disease-preventing and health-promoting properties. This herb is rich in antioxidants and dietary fiber and is a good source of minerals like potassium, calcium, manganese, iron, and magnesium. Puréeing these two nutrient-rich foods into a salad dressing is an excellent way to incorporate them into your family's diet.**

1 ripe medium avocado
¾ cup packed fresh cilantro
½ cup nonfat plain yogurt
1 garlic clove
1 tablespoon fresh lime juice
Pinch of sugar and kosher salt

Process all of the ingredients for the dressing in a blender until smooth. The dressing will keep in the refrigerator for up to 1 week.

**Makes about 1 cup**

**Tip** Another good way to serve avocado is to scoop and fork-mash it with a jar of your favorite salsa. Add a squeeze or two of fresh lime juice and serve with tortilla chips for a snack. Alice's kids call it "guaca-salsa."

# Fried Farro with Collard Greens

**Farro is a high-protein grain and a good source of fiber, vitamin E, and minerals. It is subtly sweet and nutty with a chewy texture. When paired with collard greens, this dish is nutrient packed. Add poached eggs to make a complete meal.**

1 cup farro
1 bunch collard greens, kale, or spinach
3 tablespoons olive oil
2 garlic cloves, minced
Kosher salt and freshly ground black pepper

1 Pre-toasting the farro will enhance its flavor, but you can skip this step if time is short. Preheat the oven to 375°F. Spread the farro out on a baking sheet and toast for about 10 minutes.

2 Coarsely chop the collard greens. Bring 3 cups of water to a boil, add the greens, and cook for about 5 minutes. Drain and set aside.

3 In a saucepan, combine the farro with 2½ cups salted water and bring to a boil. Lower the heat and simmer, covered, 20 to 30 minutes depending on the variety of farro. Drain well.

4 Heat the oil in a medium cast-iron skillet over medium heat. Add the garlic and cook for 1 minute. Add the farro and fry, stirring constantly, for 6 to 8 minutes until beginning to brown. Add the cooked greens and cook until heated through. Season to taste with salt and pepper. Serve immediately. Leftovers can be refrigerated and served chilled.

**Serves 4**

# Quinoa with Fennel and Pine Nuts

**Quinoa is referred to as a superfood and is considered to be a complete protein. It contains twice the protein as rice, has all nine essential amino acids, and is gluten free. Add quinoa to your table on a regular basis!**

1 cup quinoa
2 cups chicken broth or water
1½ tablespoons unsalted butter
1 large fresh fennel bulb, cut into ¼-inch cubes (about 2 cups)
Kosher salt and freshly ground black pepper
¼ cup pine nuts, toasted

1. In a large skillet, toast the quinoa over medium heat for about 5 minutes. Transfer it to a fine-mesh sieve, rinse, and drain.
2. In a large saucepan, bring the broth to a boil and add the toasted quinoa. Cover and simmer over low heat for 8 minutes.
3. Meanwhile, melt the butter in a medium cast-iron skillet over medium heat. Add the fennel cubes, salt, and pepper and sauté until almost tender, about 5 minutes. Add the fennel to the quinoa, disturbing the quinoa as little as possible. Cover and simmer 10 minutes. Stir and adjust the seasoning, if desired. If the quinoa is a little too moist, keep it covered with two layers of paper towels under the lid for a few minutes. Stir in the pine nuts and serve. This dish is good hot, at room temperature, or cold the next day.

**Serves 4 to 6**

## Variation

**Coucous with Fennel and Pine Nuts:** Couscous is grain-based and while not gluten-free, has a better vitamin profile than traditional pasta. Prepare the fennel in a large saucepan as instructed in the beginning of Step 3. Add 1 cup water with 2 cups broth and bring to a boil. Add 2 cups couscous, turn off the heat, and let stand about 10 minutes until the liquid has been absorbed. Fluff with a fork and stir in the pine nuts. Serves 4 to 6.

**Tip** Store quinoa in an airtight container in your pantry. It will keep for a longer period of time, approximately 3 to 6 months, if stored in the refrigerator.

# Desserts

# Let Them Eat Cake

**Here are mix-and-match recipes to make pretty much any cake your child desires. The basic vanilla and chocolate cake batter recipes can be doctored up with variations to make a layer cake, cupcakes, loaves, or Bundt cakes. Add the vanilla, chocolate, and/or chocolate ganache frostings for your favorite combination.**

## Classic Vanilla Layer Cake

**Layer this dense vanilla cake with rich chocolate frosting for the perfect birthday cake. Natasha just made this for her two-year-old's birthday party.**

2½ cups cake or all-purpose flour, sifted
1½ cups sugar
1 tablespoon baking powder
1 teaspoon salt
8 tablespoons (1 stick) unsalted butter, at room temperature
1 cup whole milk
1 tablespoon pure vanilla extract
2 large eggs
Favorite frosting (pages 318–319)

1 Preheat the oven to 350°F. Butter and flour two 8-inch-round cake pans.

2 In a large bowl, sift together the flour, sugar, baking powder, and salt.

3 Continue to mix, slowly adding the butter, ⅔ cup of the milk, and the vanilla. Beat vigorously.

4 Add the remaining ⅓ cup milk along with the eggs. Beat for 2 minutes, then pour into the baking pans. Bake for 30 to 35 minutes, until a toothpick inserted into the center comes out clean. (For 24 cupcakes, bake for 20 to 25 minutes; for two 9 x 5-inch loaves or one Bundt cake, bake for 40 to 45 minutes.)

5 Let the cakes cool before turning them out of the pans. When the cakes are completely cool, frost.

**Makes one 8-inch 2-layer cake**

## Variations

**Lemon Cake:** Add the finely grated zest of 1 large lemon and 1 teaspoon lemon extract.

**Orange Cake:** Add the finely grated zest of 1 orange and 1 teaspoon orange extract.

**Almond Cake:** Add 1 teaspoon almond extract for a different flavor.

# Chocolate Devil's Food Cupcakes

**This is an excellent recipe for a chocolate "from scratch" cake. The key to making a tender cake is using cake flour, which is available in the baking section of most grocery stores, and to avoid overmixing the batter. This recipe was adapted from Faye Levy's award-winning cookbook *Chocolate Sensations.***

- 2 cups cake flour
- ⅔ cup unsweetened cocoa powder
- 1¼ teaspoons baking soda
- ¼ teaspoon salt
- ½ cup buttermilk
- 12 tablespoons (1½ sticks) unsalted butter, at room temperature
- 1¾ cups sugar
- 2 large eggs
- 1½ teaspoons pure vanilla extract
- Favorite frosting (pages 318–319)

1. Preheat the oven to 350°F. Line two standard 12-cup muffin pans with paper liners.
2. In a large bowl, mix together the flour, cocoa, baking soda, and salt. In a small bowl, mix together the buttermilk and ⅓ cup water.
3. In the bowl, cream the butter with a handheld electric mixer. Add the sugar and beat until smooth. Add the eggs, one at a time, scraping down the sides of the bowl between additions. Add the vanilla and beat until well blended.

4 Slowly blend in about one-fourth of the dry ingredients, then about one-third of the wet ingredients. Repeat three times until the wet and dry ingredients are combined. Do not overmix.

5 Fill the baking cups about two-thirds full, using about ¼ cup of batter for each. Bake for approximately 20 to 25 minutes, or until a toothpick inserted into the center comes out clean. (For one 8-inch 2-layer cake, bake for 30 to 35 minutes; for two 9 x 5-inch loaves or one Bundt cake, bake for 40 to 45 minutes.)

6 Transfer the cupcakes to wire racks to cool. When cool, ice with the frosting.

**Makes 24 cupcakes**

## Variations

- Add peppermint extract and crushed candy canes to the batter make a peppermint cake.

- Add chocolate chips or a chopped chocolate bar for an extra chocolaty cake.

# Chocolate Frosting

8 tablespoons (1 stick) unsalted butter
4 squares unsweetened baking chocolate
Two 1-pound boxes confectioners' sugar
1 tablespoon pure vanilla extract
⅓ cup milk

In a small saucepan, melt the butter and chocolate together. Pour the mixture into a large bowl, add the remaining ingredients, and beat until smooth.

## Variation

**Chocolate-Hazelnut Frosting:** Mix one 13-ounce jar Nutella spread and/or 1 cup mini chocolate chips into the finished frosting.

# Chocolate Ganache Icing

**This is a more intense dark chocolate icing. It can be used as a glaze or, if whipped, as a frosting.**

8 ounces good-quality semisweet chocolate chips
½ cup heavy cream
1 teaspoon instant coffee granules

In a double boiler on the stovetop or in a microwave oven, melt the chocolate, heavy cream, and coffee together until smooth and warm, stirring occasionally. Drizzle or pour over the top of the cakes or dip cupcake tops into ganache and let set until the glaze has hardened.

# Classic Vanilla Frosting

8 tablespoons (1 stick) unsalted butter, at room temperature
Two 1-pound boxes confectioners' sugar
1 tablespoon pure vanilla extract
2 to 3 tablespoons milk or cream

In a large bowl, combine all of the ingredients and mix, either by hand or with a handheld electric mixer, until smooth. The frosting can be made in advance and refrigerated. Bring back to room temperature before using.

## Variations

**Citrus Frosting:** Instead of vanilla extract, use 1 tablespoon lemon or orange extract and the finely grated zest of 1 lemon or lime, respectively.

**Mint Frosting:** Instead of vanilla extract, use 1 tablespoon peppermint extract and ½ cup crushed candy canes or mints.

**Coconut Frosting:** Add 1¼ cups shredded, sweetened coconut to the vanilla icing and use to ice a cake or cupcakes. Spread 1¼ cups shredded, sweetened coconut onto a baking sheet and bake at 300°F until lightly toasted, 5 to 10 minutes. Let cool and sprinkle the toasted coconut on top of the iced cake or cupcakes.

# Classic Sugar Cookies

**This is a basic recipe that can be adapted many different ways. Natasha makes them with lemon zest to serve with lemonade in the summer, and rolls it out to make cookies for decorating for holidays.**

½ cup (1 stick) unsalted butter, at room temperature
½ teaspoon salt
1½ teaspoons pure vanilla extract
1¼ cups sugar
2 large eggs
2 tablespoons whole milk
2 cups all-purpose flour
1 teaspoon baking powder
½ teaspoon baking soda

1 Preheat the oven to 400°F. Lightly grease cookie sheets.

2 In a large bowl, cream together the butter, salt, vanilla, and 1 cup of the sugar. Add the eggs and milk and mix well, scraping down the bottom and sides of the bowl with a rubber spatula.

3 In a separate bowl, combine the flour, baking powder, and baking soda and gradually add to the wet ingredients. Combine well.

4 Drop the dough in mounds onto the prepared cookie sheets, 1 rounded tablespoon at a time, spacing them 2 inches apart.

5 Place the remaining ¼ cup sugar in a small bowl. Butter the bottom of a glass, dip it into the sugar, and flatten a cookie. Repeat until all of the cookies are flattened.

6 Bake for 8 to 10 minutes until light golden. Transfer the cookies to wire racks to cool.

**Makes 2½ dozen cookies**

## Variations

**Orange or Lemon Cookies:** Add 1 tablespoon finely grated orange or lemon zest to the cookie dough in Step 3.

**Snickerdoodles:** Roll the cookie dough into walnut-size balls and then roll the balls in a mixture of 2 tablespoons ground cinnamon and 2 tablespoons granulated sugar. Bake on greased cookie sheets, 2 inches apart, for 8 to 10 minutes until golden brown.

**Cutout Cookies:** Add another ½ cup flour to the dough so that it is less sticky, and stiff enough to be rolled out. Use cookie cutters to cut out the desired shapes. Decorate the cookies with sprinkles and colored sugars before baking or, once the cookies have cooled, ice and add sprinkles.

# Chocolate Chip Cookies

**There's no such thing as a kid who doesn't like chocolate chip cookies, so you can't go wrong with these in your arsenal. Adjust this recipe according to taste—nuts or no nuts, milk or dark chocolate chips. You can also double the ingredients for the cookie dough and follow Steps 1 through 3 to make enough dough for the Oatmeal Raisin Cookies on page 323.**

2¼ cups unbleached all-purpose flour
1 teaspoon baking soda
¼ teaspoon salt
¾ cup packed brown sugar
¾ cup granulated sugar
1 cup (2 sticks) unsalted butter, at room temperature
3 large eggs, slightly beaten
1 teaspoon pure vanilla extract
1 cup chopped walnuts
2 cups (24 ounces) semisweet chocolate chips

1. Preheat the oven to 375°F. Lightly grease or line baking sheets with parchment paper.
2. In a large bowl, combine the flour, baking soda, and salt and mix well.
3. In a separate bowl, combine the sugars, butter, eggs, and vanilla and mix well. Combine the two mixtures.
4. Add the nuts and chocolate chips. At this point, if you like, you can wrap and store the dough and freeze for up to 6 months.
5. Using a tablespoon, drop small mounds (you should be able to fit 16 cookies on one sheet) onto the prepared baking sheets.

6 Bake the cookies for 10 to 15 minutes until brown. Remove from the hot baking sheets immediately and transfer to wire racks to cool.

**Makes 4 dozen cookies**

## Variations

**Ice Cream Sandwiches:** Place a scoop of ice cream on a chocolate chip cookie and carefully flatten it. Top with a second cookie and press down. Roll the sides of the ice cream sandwich in chocolate chips or sprinkles. Place in a freezer bag and freeze for at least 2 hours before serving.

**Oatmeal Raisin Cookies:** Crunchy on the edges and soft in the middle, these are fast, easy, and always a hit! Omit the nuts and chocolate chips in the preceding recipe. Add 1 teaspoon ground cinnamon in Step 2, two extra teaspoons of vanilla extract in Step 3, and 2 cups rolled oats and ½ cup raisins. Bake the cookies for 10 to 15 minutes on greased cookie sheets until lightly golden for chewy oatmeal cookies, or more browned if you prefer them crispy. Cool the cookies for about 1 minute on the baking sheet before removing with a flat spatula. Makes about 4 dozen cookies.

**Ideas** Use white chocolate chips and dried cranberries in the Chocolate Chip recipe. Or omit the raisins from the Oatmeal Cookie recipe and instead add 1 cup chocolate or white chocolate chips and/or ½ cup dried cranberries. Add 1 cup chopped walnuts to either recipe.

# Brownies Like No Other

**These dense, fudgy brownies are from our friend Sasha Perl-Raver, a personal chef and caterer on the West Coast. People sigh at the mention of her brownies. Remember not to overbake them!**

1 pound (4 sticks) unsalted butter
1 pound semisweet chocolate
6 extra-large eggs, beaten
2 tablespoons pure vanilla extract
2½ cups sugar
1½ cups all-purpose flour
1 tablespoon baking powder
1 teaspoon salt
1 cup chocolate chips (semisweet, bittersweet, or milk)

1. Preheat the oven to 325°F. Grease an 18 x 12-inch baking pan.
2. Melt the butter and semisweet chocolate together in a double boiler on the stovetop. Transfer to a bowl and allow it to cool slightly but not harden. Add the eggs, vanilla, and sugar.
3. In a large bowl, sift together the dry ingredients and add to the chocolate mixture. Fold the chocolate chips into the batter.
4. Bake the brownies for 35 to 40 minutes. Do not overbake—a toothpick will not come out clean when inserted! The center should no longer be jiggly, but just slightly set, when the pan is removed from the oven. As the brownies cool, they harden up slightly and become like brownie fudge. Allow to cool completely before cutting and serving.

**Makes 16 to 20 brownies**

**Brownies with Nuts:** Add 2 cups chopped nuts and fold in with the chocolate chips.

**Peanut Butter Brownies:** Beat ½ cup creamy peanut butter into the batter, then add peanut butter chips.

**Raspberry Nut Brownies:** Add 1 cup chopped walnuts, ½ cup raspberry jam, and 1 cup fresh raspberries.

**S'mores:** Add 2 cups miniature marshmallows and 1 cup crumbled graham crackers.

**Caramel Swirl Brownies:** Swirl store-bought caramel (often sold in grocery stores as an ice cream topping) over the batter just before baking.

**Chocolate Mint Brownies:** Add 1 teaspoon mint extract to the batter.

**Candy Brownies:** M&M's are a fun, yummy addition that kids love, but just about any candy bar can be chopped up and added.

# Lemon Squares





**Natasha is our baker and treat goddess. She makes the best cupcakes, and her friends get to choose their favorite flavor combinations for their birthdays. But these lovely lemon squares are always Alice's birthday request instead of cupcakes.**

### Crust

3½ cups all-purpose flour
¼ cup confectioners' sugar
¼ teaspoon salt
1¾ cups (3½ sticks) unsalted butter, cut into bits

### Filling

6 large eggs
3 cups granulated sugar
2 tablespoons finely grated lemon zest
¾ cup freshly squeezed lemon juice
⅔ cup all-purpose flour
1 teaspoon baking powder
Confectioners' sugar for dusting

1. Preheat the oven to 350°F.
2. Make the crust: In a large bowl, sift together the flour, confectioners' sugar, and salt. Using a pastry blender or two knives, cut the butter into the flour mixture until it has the consistency of cornmeal.
3. Press the dough into a 15 x 10 x 2-inch jelly-roll pan.
4. Bake for 20 minutes, then set aside to cool.

5 While the crust is baking, make the filling: Beat the eggs until blended, then gently beat in the granulated sugar, lemon zest, lemon juice, flour, and baking powder in the order listed. Blend until smooth.

6 Pour the mixture over the cooled crust, return it to the oven, and bake for 25 minutes more.

7 Transfer the pan to a wire rack to cool. When cool, cut carefully into 2-inch squares using a sharp knife. Dust with confectioners' sugar just before serving.

**Makes about 36 squares**

# Marshmallow Rice Treats

**So why would we include a treat that you can easily find the recipe for on the side of a cereal box? Because our version is better! Slightly modified from the original over many years and many batches, this recipe produces a chewier, more buttery version that, we swear, will make people ask why yours always seem to turn out so much better than theirs. And when they do, we recommend you smile innocently and reply, "I just follow that same old recipe on the side of the box . . ."**

5 cups toasted brown-rice cereal
40 regular marshmallows, about one 10-ounce bag
3 tablespoons unsalted butter
1 teaspoon pure vanilla extract

1. Measure the cereal into a large heatproof mixing bowl. Set aside.
2. Melt the marshmallows and butter in a double boiler on the stovetop. Add the vanilla and stir until smooth.
3. Pour the melted marshmallow mixture into the bowl of cereal and stir until the cereal is evenly coated.
4. Press the mixture into an 11 x 9-inch baking pan lined with wax paper.
5. When the treats have cooled, cut into 2-inch squares and store in a sealed container.

**Makes about 2 dozen treats**

# P B & J Bars

**A snackable (and portable) version of a classic pairing. Stick 'em in their backpacks for breakfast on the go or for an afternoon snack before practice.**

2 cups uncooked rolled oats
⅓ cup creamy peanut butter
½ cup grape jelly

1. Preheat the oven to 350°F. Lightly grease an 11 x 9-inch baking pan.
2. In a medium bowl, combine all of the ingredients and mix thoroughly.
3. Spread the mixture into the prepared pan. Bake for 25 minutes. Let cool.
4. Cut into bars and wrap individually, if desired.

**Makes 8 bars**

# Apple Crisp

**Crisps are quick, comforting desserts, easily put together with the season's bounty of fresh fruit. The following basic recipe is followed by variations for fillings and toppings to transform your crisp into a cobbler or a pie.**

Filling

9 Granny Smith apples, peeled, cored, and cut into slices
Juice of 2 lemons
½ cup granulated sugar

Topping

1 cup rolled oats
1½ cups packed brown sugar
½ cup all-purpose flour
1 teaspoon ground cinnamon
½ teaspoon freshly grated nutmeg
8 tablespoons (1 stick) unsalted butter, cut into pieces
½ cup walnuts, in large pieces, or slivered almonds

1 Preheat the oven to 375°F. Make the filling: Mix together the apples, lemon juice, and sugar. Spread the filling mixture out evenly into a 13 x 9 x 2-inch baking dish.

2 Make the topping: Mix together the oats, brown sugar, flour, cinnamon, and nutmeg. Add the butter and toss it with the flour mixture. Using your fingers, rub the flour mixture and the butter together to form large crumbs. Add the nuts and toss again.

3 Sprinkle the topping mixture over the apples. Bake for about 45 minutes, or until the apples are cooked through and the top has browned. Let cool for 15 minutes. Serve warm with vanilla ice cream.

Serves 8 to 10

## Variations

**Apple-Cranberry Filling:** Substitute 2 cups fresh or frozen whole cranberries for 2 of the apples for a delicious twist on this classic.

**Peach and Berry Filling:** In a bowl, mix 7 peeled and sliced peaches, 2 pints (4 cups) fresh raspberries, ⅓ cup sugar, 2 tablespoons freshly squeezed lemon juice, and the finely grated zest of 1 lemon. Pour into a baking dish.

**Apple Crumb Pie:** Basically in this variation, you are using the same ingredients but in different proportions and with a piecrust. To make the filling: Toss 6 peeled and sliced apples with ½ cup sugar, and the juice of 1 lemon. In a separate bowl, combine 3 tablespoons all-purpose flour, 1 teaspoon ground cinnamon, ¼ teaspoon freshly grated nutmeg, and ⅛ teaspoon salt. Add the sugar-spice mixture to the apples and toss well. Pour the filling into a frozen, unbaked piecrust, mounding it slightly. To make the topping: Mix ½ cup packed brown sugar, ¾ cup all-purpose flour, 1 tablespoon ground cinnamon, ¼ teaspoon freshly grated nutmeg, and 8 tablespoons (1 stick) room-temperature unsalted butter. Using your fingers, combine until the mixture is crumbly. Sprinkle it over the apples and bake the pie at 425°F for approximately 40 minutes, or until golden brown. Serves 6 to 8.

**Fruit Cobbler:** Preheat the oven to 375°F. Mix together your favorite fruit filling and spread the mixture evenly into a 13 x 9 x 2-inch baking dish. In a bowl, mix together 2 cups all-purpose flour, 2 teaspoons baking powder, and ¾ teaspoon salt. Using a pastry blender or two knives, work in 10 tablespoons (1¼ sticks) cold unsalted butter, cut into ½-inch cubes; the mixture should have the texture of coarse bread crumbs. Stir in ¾ cup whole milk. Drop the mixture on top of the fruit filling in heaping tablespoonfuls. Sprinkle lightly with 2 tablespoons granulated sugar and bake about 40 minutes, or until nicely browned. Let cool slightly and serve. Serves 8 to 10.

# Quick Breads

**This recipe is extremely adaptable. It makes two 8- or 9-inch layers for a frosted cake, 24 cupcakes or muffins, or two 9 x 5-inch loaves. You can substitute 3 cups of grated carrots or zucchini for the bananas. Add nuts, raisins, or other chopped, dried fruit, or chocolate chips, which are particularly good with the banana and zucchini bread! You can also throw in a half cup of ground flaxseeds or wheat germ. The kids will never know it's there! Make a layer cake or cupcakes with the cream cheese frosting below or serve unfrosted as loaves or muffins for breakfast or a snack.**

1½ cups vegetable oil
1 cup granulated sugar
1 cup packed brown sugar (dark or light)
1½ cups all-purpose flour
1½ cups whole wheat flour
4 large eggs
2 teaspoons ground cinnamon
2 teaspoons baking powder
2 teaspoons baking soda
3 cups mashed ripe bananas, about 6 large bananas
1 cup unsweetened applesauce
1 teaspoon salt
1 cup chopped walnuts
1 cup raisins

1 Preheat the oven to 350°F. Grease and flour two 9-inch loaf pans and set them aside. In a large bowl, mix together the dry ingredients. In a separate bowl, mix together the wet ingredients. Combine the wet ingredients with the dry ingredients and mix well. Fold in the raisins and walnuts.

2 Pour the batter into the prepared pans and bake for 45 to 50 minutes until a toothpick inserted in the center comes out clean. Let the loaves cool in the pans for 5 minutes, then transfer them to wire racks to cool. Serve warm, or frost when completely cool. Store in airtight containers or wrap and freeze.

**Serves 8 to 10**

## Variations

**With Cream Cheese Frosting:** Using an electric mixer, blend together until fluffy: 8 ounces room-temperature cream cheese, 8 tablespoons (1 stick) room-temperature unsalted butter, 1 teaspoon pure vanilla extract, one 16-ounce box confectioners' sugar.

**Pumpkin Bars:** Eliminate the brown sugar and use 1⅔ cups granulated sugar. Use only 1 cup whole wheat flour and 1 cup all-purpose flour. Decrease the baking powder to 1 teaspoon. Use one 15-ounce can unsweetened pumpkin purée instead of the mashed bananas. The rest of the ingredients remain the same. Spread the batter out in a greased 13 x 9 x 2-inch baking pan and bake at 350°F for 25 to 30 minutes until the top of the cake springs back when touched lightly in the center or when a toothpick inserted in the center comes out clean. Cool completely, then ice with the cream cheese frosting. To serve, cut into squares.

# Ice Cream Creations

**Let's face it, there's nothing more satisfying than ice cream, even if you eat it with a spoon straight out of the container. But if you are willing to make just a little bit more of an effort, here are some great recipes to do with the lucky kids.**

## Strawberry Ice Cream Pie

1½ cups finely crushed Oreo cookie crumbs
3 tablespoons unsalted butter, melted
2 cups strawberry ice cream, softened
2 cups vanilla ice cream, softened
16 large marshmallows
16 ounces frozen strawberries, thawed, with their juice
1 cup heavy cream
¼ cup sugar

1. Mix together the cookie crumbs and butter until well combined. Press the crumbs firmly into a 10-inch pie plate and freeze for 30 minutes.
2. Fill the bottom of the chilled piecrust with strawberry ice cream. Freeze until firm, about 30 minutes.
3. Add a layer of vanilla ice cream on top of the strawberry layer. Freeze again until firm, about 30 minutes.
4. In a saucepan, combine the marshmallows with 2 to 3 tablespoons of juice from the strawberries. Stir over medium heat until melted. (Alternatively, you can coat the marshmallows with juice from the strawberries in a microwave-safe bowl and microwave on high power for about 1½ minutes, or until melted.) Set aside to cool.

5. Fold the strawberries into the cooled marshmallows. Spread the mixture onto the pie over the vanilla ice-cream layer. Freeze again until firm.
6. When you are ready to serve, whip the cream and sugar together until stiff. Spoon onto the pie and serve immediately.

Serves 6 to 8

## Banana Split

- 1 banana
- 3 scoops favorite ice-cream flavors (traditionally chocolate, vanilla, and strawberry)
- ½ cup Homemade Hot Fudge Sauce (page 339)
- 1 cup heavy cream, whipped
- 2 tablespoons chopped walnuts
- 1 maraschino cherry

1. Peel the banana and slice it lengthwise. Place the banana halves, flat side up, in the bottom of a sundae dish.
2. Add the ice cream scoops, side by side, on top of the banana. Cover with fudge sauce.
3. Garnish with the whipped cream, nuts, and top with the cherry!

Serves 2 or 3

# Make Your Own Sundaes

**Set out these homemade sauces with different ice-cream flavors, whipped cream, chopped nuts, sprinkles, etc., and let the kids go crazy!**

## Homemade Raspberry Sauce

2 cups fresh or frozen raspberries, thawed and drained
3 tablespoons sugar
1 teaspoon freshly squeezed lemon juice

Combine all of the ingredients in the bowl of a blender and blend until smooth. Strain through a fine-mesh sieve to remove the seeds, if desired. The sauce can be stored in the refrigerator for up to 2 days or frozen for up to 3 months.

Makes about 2 cups sauce

# Homemade Hot Fudge Sauce

4 ounces unsweetened chocolate
3 tablespoons unsalted butter
⅓ cup sugar
6 tablespoons corn syrup
Pinch of salt
1 tablespoon pure vanilla extract

1. Melt the chocolate and butter together in a double boiler on the stovetop or in the microwave, stirring frequently until combined.
2. Meanwhile, bring ⅔ cup water to a boil in a small, heavy saucepan. When the butter and chocolate have melted, stir them into the boiling water. Add the sugar, corn syrup, salt, and vanilla, and mix until smooth.
3. Increase the heat and stir until the mixture starts to boil; adjust the heat so that the sauce is maintained just at the boiling point for 9 minutes, stirring occasionally. Remove from heat and cool for 15 minutes. Stir in the vanilla extract.
4. Serve warm over ice cream. The sauce can be made in advance and reheated in the microwave for 15 to 30 seconds.

**Makes about 2½ cups sauce**

# A Month of Dinners

**This list of 31 dinners is for inspiration. The pairings take flavor combinations, time, and effort into consideration. In most cases, a recipe that requires more time is paired with an easy salad or steamed or roasted veggie. Or something that can be prepared in advance is paired with something that needs last-minute attention. In pairings where a starch or grain is not listed, add a side of brown or wild rice, quinoa, couscous, or whole-grain pasta. Keep in mind this important basic guideline: vegetables should be half of your plate, with grain and protein each occupying about a quarter of your plate. The list starts with lighter meals followed by chicken and fish recipes, and finishes with meats and more involved dishes that are great to freeze and repurpose.**

1. Frittata or Quiche & Creamy Tomato Soup
2. Tuscan Bean Soup & Five Star Salad
3. Empanadas or Quesadillas & Raw Vegetables with Veggie Yogurt Dip
4. Rice and Beans & Basic Roasted Vegetables
5. Macaroni and Cheese & Great Greens Sauté
6. Risotto with Zucchini and Peas & Steamed Vegetables
7. Red Peppers with Quinoa Stuffing & Asparagus with Mustard Vinaigrette
8. Southwestern Chicken Tacos & Carrot and Jicama Salad
9. Sizzling Fajitas & Avocado, Corn, and Black Bean Salsa
10. One-Dish Stir-Fry & Rice

11 Stir-Fried Tofu with Chicken and Peas & Seared Baby Bok Choy

12 Rotisserie Chicken, Smashed Red-skinned Potatoes & Sugar Snap, Radish, and Cucumber Salad

13 Chicken Fingers & Broccoli and Cauliflower Salad

14 Chicken Paprika & Sweet Potato Fries & Mashed Peas

15 Chicken with Garlic and Potatoes & Sugar Snaps with Orange-Honey Dressing

16 Ultimate Roast Chicken, Spinach Gratin & Mashed Sweet Potatoes

17 Chicken Potpie & Simple Caesar Salad

18 Broiled Salmon with Honey Dipping Sauce & Eggplant with Sesame Sauce

19 Pan-Fried Flounder, Quinoa with Fennel and Pine Nuts & Five Star Salad

20 Steamed Whole Fish & Fried Farro with Collard Greens

21 Shrimp Curry & Peas and Asparagus

22 Country-Style Ribs, Baked Sweet Potato & Quick Cabbage Slaw

23 Pork Tenderloin with Shiitake Mushrooms & Cauliflower and Apple Purée

24 Slow-Cooker Pork with Noodles & Chinese Greens with Oyster Sauce

25 Grilled to Perfection with Meats and Veggies

26 Beef Stew & Winter Vegetable Medley

27 Vegetable Lasagna & Five Star Salad

28 Turkey Shepherd's Pie & Roasted Asparagus with Parmesan

29 Turkey-Spinach Meat Loaf & Butternut Squash Purée

30 Stuffed Pasta Shells & Five Star Salad

31 Thin Linguine with Turkey Meatballs & Glazed Carrots

# Special Diets

## GLUTEN-FREE RECIPES

Gluten is a protein found in wheat (including khorasan wheat, or Kamut®, and spelt), barley, rye, malts, and triticale. It is also used as a food additive for flavoring, stabilizing or thickening in packaged or processed foods. Most of the recipes in this book are gluten free or can be adapted for gluten sensitivities. With the exception of the pancakes, waffles, muffins, bread, and dessert recipes, flour or wheat products are not a key ingredient and can be eliminated or replaced by a substitute.

Breads, pastas, grains, flour: Eliminate wheat germ when called for as a nutritional booster. Look for oat products specifically labeled gluten free (oats are frequently processed near wheat and other grains so the risk of contamination is high). Use gluten-free breads, croutons, tortillas, cereals, and granola. Use rice pasta, gluten-free pastas, and rice noodles. Use gluten-free piecrust/pastry mixes for the quiches, tarts, empanadas, and potpie recipes. Use gluten-free panko instead of bread crumbs. Eliminate flour when called for as a thickener (e.g., Chicken Potpie and Beef Stew) and use a bit of cornstarch and water instead. Farro and couscous are not gluten free. Quinoa and risotto are gluten free.

Sauces: Be careful of gluten as an additive in bottled salad dressings and sauces. Substitute tamarind sauce for soy sauce. Look for oyster sauce and fish sauce specifically labeled gluten free.

In general, make sure any prepackaged and processed foods, condiments, or canned goods you use are labeled gluten free. It is not always obvious on ingredient lists. For example, energy bars may be processed on a conveyer belt dusted with flour to prevent sticking. Many processed meats (bacon, cold cuts, sausages, hot dogs) contain gluten as a binding agent. Rotisserie chickens may be seasoned with spices that contain gluten, so be sure to check with your grocer.

## LACTOSE-FREE RECIPES

Lactose intolerance is the inability to metabolize lactose, a sugar found in milk. Milk, butter, yogurt, cheese, or cream are not key ingredients in many of the recipes in this book and can be replaced by a substitute or eliminated. (Note that eggs, found in the dairy section, are naturally lactose free.) In most cases, you can use oil, dairy-free margarine, or buttery spreads in place of butter in cooking; lactose-free milk, soy milk, rice milk, or nondairy creamer for the milk; lactose-free yogurt instead of regular yogurt. There can be lactose in packaged breads, cereals, or granola, and even in processed meats such as sausage, bacon, lunch meats, and hot dogs, so be sure to look for "dairy-free" labels. With the exception of Quick Breads, the dessert recipes in this book are not lactose free and are not tested for baking with nondairy substitutes.



## Table of Equivalents

The exact equivalents in the following tables have been rounded for convenience.

LIQUID/DRY MEASURES

| U.S. | METRIC |
|---|---|
| ¼ teaspoon | 1.25 milliliters |
| ½ teaspoon | 2.5 milliliters |
| 1 teaspoon | 5 milliliters |
| 1 tablespoon (3 teaspoons) | 15 milliliters |
| 1 fluid ounce (2 tablespoons) | 30 milliliters |
| ¼ cup | 60 milliliters |
| ⅓ cup | 80 milliliters |
| ½ cup | 120 milliliters |
| 1 cup | 240 milliliters |
| 1 pint (2 cups) | 480 milliliters |
| 1 quart (4 cups, 32 ounces) | 960 milliliters |
| 1 gallon (4 quarts) | 3.84 liters |
| 1 ounce (by weight) | 28 grams |
| 1 pound | 454 grams |
| 2.2 pounds | 1 kilogram |

OVEN TEMPERATURES

| Fahrenheit | Celsius | Gas |
|---|---|---|
| 250 | 120 | ½ |
| 275 | 140 | 1 |
| 300 | 150 | 2 |
| 325 | 160 | 3 |
| 350 | 180 | 4 |
| 375 | 190 | 5 |
| 400 | 200 | 6 |
| 425 | 220 | 7 |
| 450 | 230 | 8 |
| 475 | 240 | 9 |
| 500 | 260 | 10 |

LENGTHS

| U.S. | METRIC |
|---|---|
| ⅛ inch | 3 millimeters |
| ¼ inch | 6 millimeters |
| ½ inch | 12 millimeters |
| 1 inch | 2.5 centimeters |

# Index

Published in 2012 by Welcome Books®
An imprint of Welcome Enterprises, Inc.
6 West 18th Street, New York, NY 10011
(212) 989-3200; Fax (212) 989-3205
www.welcomebooks.com

Publisher: Lena Tabori
Project Director: Alice Wong
Designer: H. Clark Wakabayashi

Text by Alice Wong and Natasha Tabori Fried; sidebar text contribution by Ellen Leach. Illustration Credits: C.M. Burd: page 42; Ellen Clapsaddle: 55; E. Curtis: 65, 274, 277, 301, 306; P. Ebner: 273; Maud Humphrey: 39, 267; Rosie O'Neil: 84, 85, 193; Maxfield Parrish: 187; Margaret Evans Price: 145; Jessie Willcox Smith: 102-103, 219, 248, 305.



Library of Congress Cataloging-in-Publication data on file.

ISBN 978-1-59962-109-8
First Edition
Printed in China
1 3 5 7 9 10 8 6 4 2

For more information about this book, please visit:
www.welcomebooks.com/littlebigcookbookformoms

If you notice an error please check the website where there will hopefully be a posted correction. If not, please alert us by emailing info@welcomebooks.com and we will post a correction.